How Political Correctness Weakens Schools

How Political Correctness Weakens Schools

Stop Losing and Start Winning Educational Excellence

Jim Dueck

ROWMAN & LITTLEFIELD
Lanham • Boulder • New York • London

Published by Rowman & Littlefield
A wholly owned subsidiary of The Rowman & Littlefield Publishing Group, Inc.
4501 Forbes Boulevard, Suite 200, Lanham, Maryland 20706
www.rowman.com

Unit A, Whitacre Mews, 26-34 Stannary Street, London SE11 4AB

Copyright © 2016 by Jim Dueck

All rights reserved. No part of this book may be reproduced in any form or by any electronic or mechanical means, including information storage and retrieval systems, without written permission from the publisher, except by a reviewer who may quote passages in a review.

British Library Cataloguing in Publication Information Available

Library of Congress Cataloging-in-Publication Data Available
ISBN 978-1-4758-2986-0 (cloth : alk. paper)
ISBN 978-1-4758-2987-7 (pbk. : alk. paper)
ISBN 978-1-4758-2988-4 (electronic)

∞™ The paper used in this publication meets the minimum requirements of American National Standard for Information Sciences—Permanence of Paper for Printed Library Materials, ANSI/NISO Z39.48-1992.

Printed in the United States of America

Contents

Preface vii

Introduction ix

1 Learning Well and Living Well 1
2 Low Expectations Provide for Mediocre Education 11
3 Moving from Intuition to Intelligence 25
4 Harnessing Power through Comparability 41
5 Choice: A Democratic Right 57
6 Coaches Are Not Evaluators 65
7 Birth Rather Than Worth Matters Too Much 79
8 Teachers' Professional Development 97
9 Reducing Administration Costs 103
10 Maximizing Students' Work Year 109
11 Unions Belong in the Accountability Tent 117
12 Accountability for University Departments of Education 129
13 Job-for-Life Is a Wrong Practice 139
14 Rewarding Performance 151
15 Holding Parents Accountable 159

16 Reducing Unfairness to Students	165
17 Meeting the Costs	169
Summary of Recommendations	173
References	177
About the Author	183

Preface

Forty years in the education system as teacher, principal, superintendent, and then assistant deputy minister responsible for implementing accountability in a provincial school system made me acutely aware of the plethora of issues requiring understanding by both workers in the system as well as its users. Avoiding political risks associated with bringing these issues into the public arena for discussion typifies the government's usual response opting, instead, to throw more money into the system believing that the public will *measure its leadership performance by how much is spent rather than how well students achieve.*

Three previous books—*Being Fair with Kids, Educations' Flashpoints,* and *Common Sense about Common Core*—provide considerable research and data supporting a need *to transform education* so that students, who cannot vote, rather than educators, who can vote, *sit atop education's pyramidal pinnacle.* Political correctness must be challenged on many issues in our school system so that our children have a better chance for *learning well* and then *living well.*

Education for this generation's youth is the key to our nation's future well-being, which is now threatened. This book presents a plan *for winning in a global village* where traditional economic conditions are being overturned; however, the pathway outlined runs counter to the best interests of teachers' unions who pursue their members' ultimate objective: *less work with more pay.*

Less work is a complex issue dealing with more than working during hours, days, and years. Class size, for example, is an issue teachers have cleverly portrayed as a learning rather than a working condition. North American governments in particular have expended significant sums of money to reduce class size; however, this *input* has failed us and political correctness will find it difficult to amend their failure. The "horse is out of the barn" and recovering wasted funding will experience overwhelming resistance.

This book's focus is on using accountability to *pressure the system* toward implementing reforms necessary for winning. Applying accountability throughout all levels of the education system signals the important message that outcomes matter and that students rather than teachers should sit atop the pyramidal pinnacle. Such a focus on educational outcomes replaces the current culture too dominated with its focus on inputs such as spending and job satisfaction.

These comments should not be interpreted as antiunion. They fulfill the valuable function of representing people who may feel somewhat insecure that their service is valued. I loved teaching and working in schools where I could experience directly the difference being made in students' lives. My issue is with *forcing* people to be a union member in order to work and with unions having the power to take advantage of their *monopolistic environment* through strike action.

Hence, the problem originates and continues to exist with governments who carelessly spend our money on the pretext that they will use it to improve education. In fact, their motivation is selfish because they know that the public does not understand the complexities within education and they *avoid bringing information forward to inform parents and taxpayers*. Lack of transparency helps politicians secure votes from educators, who are the largest block of workers in our society, while hiding the negative impact on our students.

This book deals with educational policies, which are controversial and also identified by others for being problematic, *rather than just classroom practices*. Fairness to students is a significant concern shared by many whose perspectives are included; however, these references are not exhaustive by any means. The solutions, or recommendations, proposed are intended to ensure that policies align with the best interests of education's clients—students, parents, and taxpayers—rather than those of the service providers.

Introduction

This book begins with a discussion regarding the important role education plays in a country's capacity to be successful in our global village. The focus then shifts to demonstrating how homes and schools are failing both Canada and the United States for future success because standards and expectations are declining. A politically correct environment seeks to avoid controversial issues by maintaining the status quo on matters related to workers in the education system while avoiding the best interests of the school system's clients.

The problem can be summed by referring to education's pyramidal pinnacle and discovering which group sits atop and why this is so. It should be students but it is not, because politicians know that educators comprise the largest workforce in our society and that their votes can be the difference between which government is in power and which is not. On the other hand, students cannot vote and it is easy to relegate them to lower levels in the pyramid because they lack understanding of how they are disadvantaged.

Each provides a summary of a condition within education that demonstrates how the well-being of students is subjugated for the benefit of the educator's service providers. These summaries are not exhaustive because a book could be devoted about each; however, sufficient evidence is presented to provide readers with a basic understanding of how the issue is unfair to students.

Exposing these issues is helpful to readers who work within the school system, or are parents with children served by the school system, or are taxpayers expecting that their dollars will provide maximum return on investment. Recommendations proposing how the existing paradigm can be changed for the benefit of students are imbedded within each discussion and summarized at the conclusion of the book.

An extensive listing of references concludes the book, which provides readers with additional perspectives and research. This listing demonstrates that the issues identified are not merely this author's personal musings but a concern to many others desiring an effective and efficient education system.

Chapter 1

Learning Well and Living Well

The conundrum about which comes first, the chicken or the egg, has attracted attention for many decades. The question tantalizes us because there is no obvious conclusion and it engages people who enjoy meandering through philosophical thought. Wikipedia explains this metaphor by stating that "cultural references to the chicken and egg intend to point out the futility of identifying the first case of a *circular cause and consequence*." For most, debating this question would be irrelevant. For some, a conclusion is important because of the logic required.

Effective schools and a *productive society* provide a similar circular reference because a relationship is evident, but there is difficulty in calculating the relative impact of one variable on the other. One perspective is that schools are the training ground for the next generation's leaders, workers, and citizens. *An ill-prepared generation is unable to provide the ingredients for a productive society.*

The other perspective in the circular cause and sequence is that without a productive society in place, expectations for our school system are insufficiently low. People who have traveled before us can refine what is, and demand more of what should be, in order for them to reap the benefit in their later years. If the training ground is weak, the consequences will tap into the well-being of those living in retirement.

While it is not essential that this issue be resolved, the context of this book is that schools provide the training ground for renewing society. Attitudes and abilities imparted to students—the next generation of parents, workers, and voters—have a profound impact on how well our society performs. We are wise in focusing attention to the myriad of issues evident in how our schools facilitate the development of our young citizens on whom our future depends. Hence, *learning well, living well*, is a meaningful slogan in this discussion.

Focusing on the important role that schools play in our society is not intended to demean the critical role of the home. Examining the various domains in child development underscores the home's importance for a nation's well-being, and a critical message in this book pertains to *a necessity for there to be a strong partnership between the home and the school.*

SHIFTING MANDATE IN CHILD DEVELOPMENT

Perhaps the best way to explain this school and home partnership is to establish who has primary responsibility for each of the child's developmental areas. The home, for example, has primary responsibility for the child's spiritual development. Parents may choose to register their child in a school that can support the parents' spiritual aspirations by providing religious instruction consistent with their beliefs. In our society, such a partnership is usually confined to a private institution where parents pay some to all costs for education.

For example, Tompson et al. (2013) report on the question, "How would you rate the quality of education in US public schools?" Parents whose children attend private schools are more likely than parents of public school children to say *their* child's school (91 percent vs. 75 percent) and private schools in the United States (88 percent vs. 57 percent) are "good" or "excellent."

Many decades ago the school system routinely accommodated a spiritual emphasis and it was usual for the school day to begin with the Lord's Prayer and some reading from the Bible. Indeed, portions of the Bible—that is, the New Testament—were freely distributed to students, and Christian clubs operated within many public schools. These activities were intended to provide support to parents who wanted their children equipped with a belief system that provided a skeleton to which morals and values could be attached.

An emerging pluralistic society negated school activities associated with one religion, and the education system inculcated teaching morals and values into the curriculum without making religious inferences. Respecting oneself includes respecting others and all that is in the world around us. *As desirable as this is, it is unnecessary to provide documentation regarding the degree to which respect for each other is deteriorating.* Antibullying programs are now a dominant feature in all walks of life. Everyone has experienced road rage. Mass shootings are too common an occurrence. Politicians seeking electoral success demean opponents.

Lack of respect for others also translates into increasing dishonesty. During a conversation with an owner of a gasoline service station, who employs up to twenty-five high school students at one time, he spoke disparagingly of the lack of standards in his young workforce. Not only was there a lack of pride in their dress and work ethic, but *theft was a major concern*. In his conversations with others in this large, worldwide gasoline distribution enterprise, which features many cash transactions, he discovered that dishonest behavior is now pandemic throughout the industry.

Compelling evidence about dishonesty is now also evident within the education system. Eli Newberger (1999) compared data from the 1940s and found that in a 1997 survey of high achievers in high school, 87 percent judged cheating to be "common" among their peers. Seventy-six percent confessed they themselves had cheated. By way of contrast, a national sample of US college students in the 1940s found that only 20 percent admitted to cheating in high school when they were questioned anonymously. Cheating is considerably more prevalent today, and contrary to some people's opinion, *cheating is not restricted to weak students attempting to improve their chances at passing*.

Niels (2014) researched the major reasons why students cheat and published his results online on the website About.com (January 17, 2014). His research led him to believe that students cheated for the following reasons:

1. There is a mechanism within each of us which triggers a need to "save face." Saving face can mean a desire to save oneself from the angry assault of a parent or a teacher.
2. Cheating is no longer deviant behavior but normal behavior because everybody does it.
3. Cheating offers an easy way out. Why bother studying hard and doing all those term papers by yourself if you can use someone else's work?

Niels's findings support the notion that cheating can occur with students of *every ability level whenever they perceive the need to get ahead without expending the necessary effort*. These findings also imply that the odds of being caught are relatively small and that the school system has inadequate safeguards in place.

Newberger also verifies that the odds of getting away with academic cheating are heavily weighted in the cheater's favor. "Ninety percent of the confessed cheaters surveyed by *Who's Who* said they had never been caught. . . . *The incentive has changed from passing by the weak student to getting into select universities by the stronger students*."

The school system is on weakening ground, however, when it attempts to deal with student cheating. An investigation by the Georgia Bureau of Investigation released in July 2011 found that 44 out of 56 Atlanta schools cheated on the 2009 Criterion-Referenced Competency Tests. In their efforts to meet targets set by the district and avoid a negative evaluation or termination if they did not, 178 teachers and principals were found to have corrected wrong test answers entered by students. The size of the scandal has been described as one of the largest in US history.

Educators, too, have an excuse for yielding to pressure from improvement targets as stipulated in the US government's No Child Left Behind (NCLB) Act, by pointing to a national scandal involving state administrators. A study by the US Department of Education indicated that the observed differences in states' reported test scores were largely due to differences in the stringency of their standards on state-wide tests.

By 2009, Grade 4 reading tests of all states demonstrated that their "proficient standard" was below America's national testing program equivalent. States could have selected the national testing program known as the *National Assessment of Educational Progress* (NAEP); however, they would have *lost the ability to manipulate* the standards. State administrators may have felt offended by this being labeled *cheating*; however, their motivation was to ensure more schools met their goals and received additional federal funding without improving student achievement. *The public purse was defrauded by this manipulation.*

States manipulated their tests for their own gain, both monetarily and in public perception. None of the states established a proficiency level on their tests that was higher than the proficiency level on the national test. Given the huge discrepancies in student achievement across the country, it is logical that national proficiency standards should be exceeded by expectations for proficiency on many state tests. For most states, their proficiency level was actually below the national test's *basic level. NCLB failed to take into account the tendency of people to employ whatever means is necessary to pursue the end (more funding) that is desired.*

The point in this discussion pertaining to the spiritual domain in child development is that adhering to a moral code for a productive society is not maintaining previous standards. Promoting Christian values, once a norm in North American education, in a pluralistic society is now politically incorrect. Even educators are stepping outside of legal lines. Lacking a spiritual emphasis in education is hindering our children from locating the "magnetic north pole" in their moral compass. *The end is now justifying the means.* It does not matter whether methods are legal or illegal, fair or foul, kind or cruel, honest or dishonest.

A clear message from home gives children something to return to, as well as to push against as they grow and develop their own internal compass. The task was made easier when the child's place of learning, the school, reinforced the home's instruction. Society reinvents itself through the school system and, without a spiritual component in place, Christian values are in decline. The Golden Rule—do unto others as you want them to do unto you—is in retreat.

Debating *circular cause and consequence within the spiritual domain* will produce strongly held conflicting views but, as another popular saying goes, "This horse has left the barn." The clock will not be turned back. Political correctness will prevail and society will reap the consequences both good and bad.

SHARED MANDATES

Focusing on other domains in child development, a *partnership* with parents having primary responsibility with support from the school is evident in the physical, social/emotional, and adaptive domains. At least this is how early schooling was envisioned. Societal changes are occurring and schools are experiencing *mandate creep* in these domains. Anderson (2013) reports that, in the United States, the number of children living in single-parent homes has nearly doubled since 1960, according to data from the 2010 Census. Anderson points out that:

> *The Washington Times* analyzed the most recent census data, showing that the percentage of two-parent families has dropped significantly over the past decade in all 50 states. Even as the total number of American households with children increased by 160,000, the number of two-parent households decreased by 1.2 million.
>
> Today, *one-third of American children*—a total of 15 million—are being raised *without* a father. Nearly five million more children live *without* a mother. *A growing number of studies show that fatherlessness has a major negative impact on the social and emotional development of children.* A 2011 University of Melbourne study found that absent fathers were linked with higher rates of juvenile delinquency, while a Canadian study showed that kids whose fathers were active parents in early and middle childhood had fewer behavior problems and higher intellectual abilities as they grew older, even among socio-economically at-risk families. Children without fathers are much more likely to grow up in poverty. While married couples with children enjoy an average income of $80,000, single mothers average only $24,000.

Such a dramatic shift in the home's demographics impact our children in negative ways. There are now considerable challenges associated with raising children into the kind of men and women we want them to become. While there are always noteworthy exceptions, experiences from many years in school administration provide sufficient evidence that single parenting is a more challenging role.

In the physical domain, lifestyle changes have created a significant change in our children's physical well-being. Physical activity was not a concern during the agrarian era; however, lack of exercise leading to obesity is a significant issue in this generation. The Alliance for a Healthier Generation website identifies several reasons why children are prone to being obese:

- Television and Media: Screen time is a major factor contributing to childhood obesity. It takes away from the time children spend being physically active, leads to increased snacking in front of the TV, and influences children with advertisements for unhealthy foods.
- Lack of Daily Physical Activity: Most adolescents fall short of the Physical Activity Guidelines for Americans recommendation of at least sixty minutes of aerobic physical activity every day. Only 18 percent of students in Grades 9 through 12 met this recommendation in 2007. Daily, quality physical education in school can help students meet the guidelines; however, in 2009 only 33 percent had access to and attended daily physical education classes.
- Increased Portion Sizes: Portion sizes of less healthy foods and beverages have increased over time in restaurants, grocery stores, and vending machines. Research shows that children eat more without realizing it if they are served larger portions. This means they are consuming a lot of extra calories, especially when eating high-calorie foods.
- Higher Consumption of Sugary Beverages: Sugary drinks are the largest source of added sugar in the diets of children and adolescents. Increasing consumption of these high-calorie beverages that offer little or no nutrients is associated with the increasing rates of childhood obesity. Research reports that one-fifth of teens eat the equivalent of an extra meal in sugar-sweetened beverages.

Schools inherited a societal need and parental primary responsibility to address physical concerns in our youth by placing greater emphasis on physical activity. Since children without fathers are much more likely to grow up in poverty because single mothers average only $24,000 in income annually, many children are excluded from participating in costly community programs where physical activity is featured. The school's mandate has shifted, *but accommodating this societal concern was not accompanied with an increase in school time.* Additional time for physical activity was recovered from what is frequently referred to as academic programming.

In the social/emotional domain, family break-up is impacting the important understandings children acquire from having both a mother and father. Much learning can be acquired from watching two adults work as a *team* while effectively resolving conflicts when differences in opinion occur. These are important abilities when children move into adulthood and have their own children, or when they are part of a workplace team.

A poignant illustration of this is evident in Canada's early treatment of its aboriginal population, when children were removed from the home and placed in residential schools. Such minimal interaction with their parents, which lasted for several decades, resulted in a generation of parents ill-equipped to handle the parenting role once residential schools were deemed a failure and disbanded.

Having not interacted with parents but now being parents, a profound gap in social development is evident as many aboriginal families grapple with serious problems in their children. Physical and substance abuse combined with gang behavior are tragic outcomes resulting in high incidences of suicide. Canadian society is experiencing the negative consequences of a policy where First Nations' children were *not* able to live and connect with their parents. In this instance, interaction with *both* parents was denied.

School principals have to be mindful of the social implications when the male role model is absent in the home. The *Washington Times* report above articulates negative consequences in juvenile delinquency as well as increased levels of discipline problems and decreased levels of student achievement in single-parent homes. Principals are mindful of this issue when they establish class lists for a new school year, especially since the vast majority of teachers are female. Principals frequently express their intent to provide a male role model for specific students in the classroom to compensate the lack of such an influence in the home.

The point in drawing attention to these societal issues is to demonstrate how domains in children's development, once the primary responsibility of the parents with support from the school, are now less clearly delineated. In other words, *the school's mandate is expanded because the family is less able to provide adequate care for their children.* The outcome of this change is that there is now an additional threat to the slogan that proposes a relationship between *learning well and living well*.

SCHOOL MANDATES

Two remaining domains—that is communicative and cognitive—in child development are the long-standing, *primary* responsibility of the education system with support from the home. The former domain deals with a child's skills to understand the spoken word and express himself or herself verbally. Acquiring these skills begin early in a child's life before schooling; however, sophistication occurs as the student progresses through the grades and into postsecondary education. The ability to comfortably speak and comprehend complex sentences is an important skill in the workplace, especially in leadership roles.

Cognitive development for learning and thinking is another domain that is the primary responsibility of the school and supported by the home. This domain represents the myriad programs of study in the school curriculum related to academic studies including technology. In this domain, training occurs to ready students for success in the world of work as well as for being a productive member of our society. We know these skills, knowledge, and understandings to be the key responsibility of the school system because, when we actually endeavor to measure school performance, these are the focus.

The purpose of this chapter is to examine responsibility in the process of developing our children for success in an increasingly complex world. A critical message in this process is that the schools' role in preparing children for adulthood is *expanding* because the home is flagging in its role to provide key training. Educators frequently lament the new reality by referencing how strong the support was in the bygone era when a phone call to the home would produce effective reinforcement, leading to the child's immediate change to more positive behavior.

Learning well, living well is a slogan that has served us well, but the home's shift away from fulfilling its roles is weakening our potential. The long-standing partnership between the home and the school is increasingly tenuous as parents struggle in their roles. The public now is hoping that the school system can expand its mandate and assume greater responsibility for developing our future leaders, workers, and citizens to be productive members of our society.

Avoiding any reference to problems emanating from a deteriorating home environment is the politically correct response, but such disregard for the essential role contributed by parents will not auger well in achieving meaningful reform. Compensating for the social implications of a weakened partner in the home/school relationship places added burden on our school system; yet, time in school to accomplish the expanded mandate is not increased. Actually, schools are borrowing time from what was traditionally their mandate.

At the same time, the next chapter will demonstrate that the education system struggles to achieve its mandate. Perhaps the struggle is related to difficulties that parents are experiencing or is it possible that the school system is insufficient in providing students with the skills, knowledge, and understandings necessary to contribute to our slogan of *learning well, living well*?

KEY POINTS

- An ill-prepared generation is unable to provide the ingredients for a productive society.
- Schools provide the training ground for renewing society; however, spiritual development is no longer accommodated in public schooling and is the parent's exclusive responsibility.

- Respect for each other is deteriorating and translates into increasing dishonesty.
- The moral code for a productive society is not maintaining previous standards.
- The physical, social/emotional, and adaptive domains are a shared mandate with parents having primary responsibility.
- Two domains—that is communicative and cognitive—in child development are the primary responsibility of the education system with support from the home.
- The schools' role in preparing children for adulthood is expanding because the home is flagging in its role to provide key training.
- *Learning well, living well* is a slogan that has served us well, but the home's shift away from fulfilling its roles is weakening our potential.

Chapter 2

Low Expectations Provide for Mediocre Education

Learning well, living well, like the chicken and the egg, is a *circular cause and consequence* issue. Within the *learning well* aspect, the previous chapter reveals that the partnership between the home and our schools is experiencing an unwelcome mandate shift with the breakdown of the family unit placing additional burden on the education system. Chapter 15 in this book outlines the dramatic shift required within our school system to increase parental accountability and tackle the negative consequences arising from this shifting mandate.

This chapter's focus is on the other side of the equation in the *circular cause and consequence* issue: *learning well* as determined through our school system's success. Learning well is the product of an interplay between the home and the school, and the data story for the education system regarding success in achieving its mandate for learning well is *cause for concern*.

The public is too frequently lead astray by politicians who emphasize inputs rather than outcomes. When confronted with a concern, too many leaders select *throwing more money* at the concern. Voters are conditioned to measure quality by how much funding is allocated to an area and, when a problem is identified, believe politicians have the right approach when pledging to increase funding. Spending, or an input, is more readily understood and measured than determining success using outcomes, and dangerously high levels of government debt is now a catastrophic result of this approach.

Expectations are a perennial political issue, and education is no exception: indeed, it may be the epitome of how the public can be misled. When the public focus is on inputs, such as spending more money, pressure to produce results is reduced. *Expectations are related to accountability*, which usually generates opposition from special interest groups who, in the case of education, include the educators represented by their unions.

IMPACT OF TEACHERS' UNIONS

The union's fundamental purpose is the pursuit of *less work with more pay* for its members. This expression is not a negative one and it should not be a surprise. Workers organize into unions to have someone negotiate their pay and working conditions with an expectation that they will achieve the best possible outcomes. Teachers' unions are, if not the most successful, certainly one of the most effective at negotiating the best for their members.

At his retirement speech in 2009, Bob Chanin, former general counsel for the National Educators' Association (NEA), spoke about his union's success:

> I have found it increasingly necessary to spend time defending NEA and its affiliates against attacks from government agencies, conservative and right-wing groups and unfriendly media. Why you may ask is this so? Why are these conservative and right-wing bastards picking on NEA and its affiliates? I will tell you why. It is the price we pay for success. NEA and its affiliates have been singled out because they are the most effective union in the United States. . . . It is not because we care about children. And it is not because we have a vision of a great public school for every child. NEA and its affiliates are effective advocates because we have power. *And we have power because there are more than 3.2 million people who are willing to pay us hundreds of millions of dollars in dues each year.*

From a political perspective, teachers' unions have emerged as powerful forces in educational politics. People are now more likely to understand that *unions are there to support the best interests of their members*. The controversy surrounding these unions is whether they are a *stumbling block to reform* or *advocates for better schools and better teachers*. Public attitudes regarding this differing perspective are shifting. Peterson et al. (2012) asked Americans the question, "Do you think *teacher unions* have a generally positive effect on schools, or do you think they have a generally negative effect?"

While 41 percent of the public selected the neutral position, those with a positive view of unions dropped to 22 percent in 2012 from 29 percent in 2011. The survey question is loaded with conflicting values which likely influence such a high rate of uncertainty with two out of five Americans indicating a neutral position. There may also be some ambivalence because many Americans do not have a recent connection with the school system and, in their mind, rephrased the "neutral" option as "I don't know."

The survey's most striking finding was "that 58 percent of teachers took a positive view of unions in 2011, and only 43 percent did in 2012. The number of teachers holding negative views of unions nearly doubled to 32 percent from 17 percent." A change of this magnitude in one year must be a substantial concern to union leadership. Initially, unions supported the US Common

Core initiative but, as the focus shifted from acquiring learning standards to using test results in teacher evaluations, were teachers telling their unions to back away?

Everyone wants higher levels of public sector accountability until it enters their own backyard. Accountability is assigned to services we *value*, and we want *assurances* that high standards are maintained. Education meets these criteria; yet, educators shy away from the opportunity to provide services where high standards are the norm. Rather than considering accountability as recognition for a job well done, resistance is the adopted position.

Skepticism toward teachers' unions is also voiced by high-profile people in government. With concerns regarding failing schools running high, Jerry Adler (2010) with Newsweek coordinated a debate about the role America's unions play and their image of being intransigent while defending every teacher. Rod Paige, former US secretary of education provided his blunt assessment of teachers' union power:

> Teachers' unions represent the *most dominant political force in American education*—highly financed, highly organized, mammoth organizations. The National Education Association has 3.2 million members, 14,000 locals, and in 2007 they collected about $400 million from their members. In America about 12 percent of the workforce is unionized, but *in education it's 38 percent*. Teachers' unions sit on both sides of the negotiating table in many cases. They have representatives on the school boards, so they're negotiating with themselves. *You heard a lot about children. Don't be fooled: teacher's unions' main interest is the welfare of their members.*

Secretary Paige not only underscores the perception that unions are there for their members and not for their clients, but he also raised the specter of a conflict of interest where people with direct ties to education sit on school boards. *Governments and their citizens pay dearly for their unwillingness to confront this irregularity.*

Canada's situation is not dissimilar to that of the United States. Black (2013), an example of Chanin's "unfriendly media," looks at the other side of this coin and succinctly describes how teacher unionization in Canada progressed successfully in the public sector.

> For many years, the often explicit understanding was that public employees would be less well-paid than those in the private sector, but would have greater job security and, in general, less challenging employment. The unionization of the public service consigned that rule of thumb to the proverbial dust-bin of history, and public-service unions began leading organized labour in militancy, while feasting on the weakness and cowardice of political employers. . . . It is now a familiar three-hanky tear-jerker to see teachers' union representatives

passionately explaining that the last thing they wish to do by striking in the middle of the school year is hold the students hostage or impinge on the money-earning capacity of their parents; but that is, of course, what they are doing and why they are doing it.

In the education sector, the union's success is too frequently downplayed because the public's representatives are politicians who also want votes at election time. Educators are the largest employee group in our society representing approximately 3 percent of voters, and when family members, who feel the impact of the collective agreements of teachers' unions are included, there is *considerable pressure on politicians to reduce expectations by yielding to demands during negotiations.*

In a pyramidal relationship involving educators, students, parents, and taxpayers, governance too frequently places educators at the top. Verbalizing support for teachers without referencing and acknowledging the power of their unions is a politically correct option for someone seeking election.

The needs of each group in the pyramid are important and require thoughtful consideration; however, in the context of *learning well, living well,* the primary focus must be on *students.* The overwhelming majority cannot vote, and it is fallacious to believe that the people who serve them as educators have the capacity to set aside their self-interests for those of their clients. As educators we may be well intentioned, but we still retain biases dominated by self-interest, and these are readily apparent whenever concepts related to accountability emerge.

The foregoing discussion regarding the union's success at the bargaining table is important in this chapter because it assists our understanding regarding why our school system is failing to meet expectations. *We should expect a return on investment commensurate with an increase in funding.* Our politicians should be pouring taxpayers' dollars into a public enterprise for a better reason than acquiring votes for reelection. *Educational outcomes should be improving with increased funding, and we should confront our politicians when their decisions fail to produce such outcomes.*

EDUCATION'S RETURN ON INVESTMENT IS LAGGING

Governments periodically release reports regarding the state of their education system to stimulate reform. In the United States, the 1983 release of *A Nation at Risk* report was a landmark event that unsettled the educational system. In memorable language, it stated that, *If an unfriendly foreign power had attempted to impose on America the mediocre educational performance that exists today, we might well have viewed it as an act of war.* Such a graphic description of failure left an unsuspecting citizenry and vested interest groups incensed, and many subsequent statements sought to reassure the public that all was well.

Almost all of the world's major economies participate in data-gathering activities conducted by the Organisation for Economic Co-operation and Development (OECD). Figure 2.1 from this organization demonstrates the level of educational spending per pupil in 2007, immediately prior to the 2008 world recession. This level of spending is relevant because it represents the period when students attended school preceding international assessments.

Excluding Luxembourg, which includes preschool expenditures in their data, the United States is a *big spender* in education. Americans value education and spend *47 percent more* than the OECD average. This is great news for people who like to *measure how much money is spent*. A more important issue is the impact that spending has on outcomes such as student achievement measured by test scores.

Despite high levels of spending, American students' performance on international tests such as The International Study of Science and Mathematics (TIMSS), Progress in International Reading Literacy Study (PIRLS), and Programme for International Student Assessment (PISA) clearly demonstrate

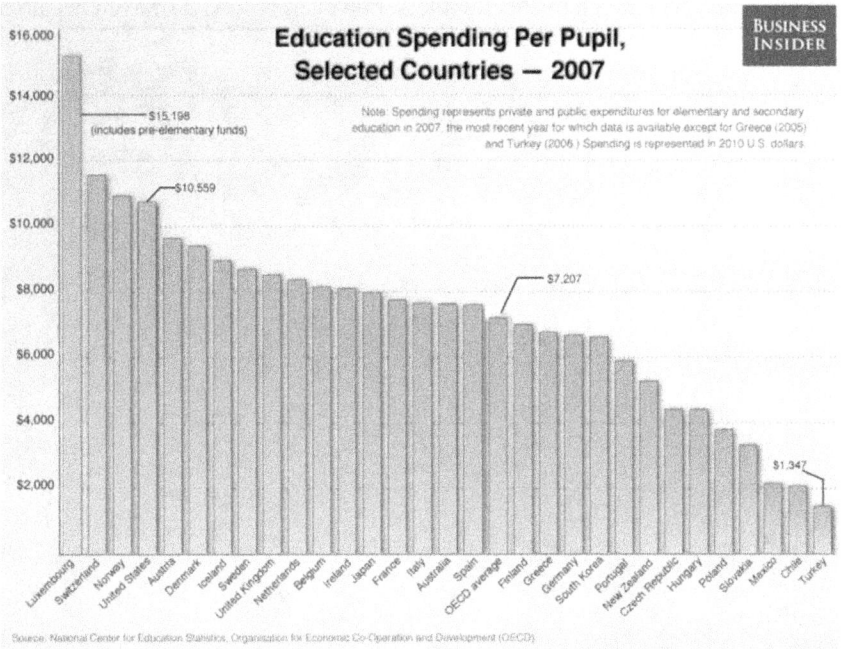

Figure 2.1   Education Spending Per Pupil in Selected Countries- 2007

that the *United States is at risk*. This chapter's focus is on the school's contribution in the *circular cause and consequence* issue related to *learning well, living well*. Learning well is the product of an interplay between the home and the school, and the data story for the US education system regarding success in achieving its mandate *was suspect and remains so*.

These international tests assess students' ability to demonstrate learning for cognitive outcomes identified across the world, which can be measured by paper/pencil tests. In a sense, *these assessments represent a common core of outcomes or standards for the world without stipulating a common curriculum*. Other outcomes such as listening, speaking, creativity, collaboration, etc., frequently identified as "softer skills," require more individualized assessment procedures and are not incorporated in these tests.

McKinsey and Company analyzed 2003 international mathematics test scores in figure 2.2 (by Googling "spending on education by country") and analyzed these scores relative to *spending per student per point*. In other words, using the score for each American student writing the test, they determined *how much money was expended to score one point*. The most money expended could identify *the least effective expenditure of education funding* and, in such an analysis, the average US expenditure was $165 per point or *59 percent more* than the average participating country.

This factoid provides those people who like to measure government spending (an input) with much to cheer. Others, however, will be dismayed because

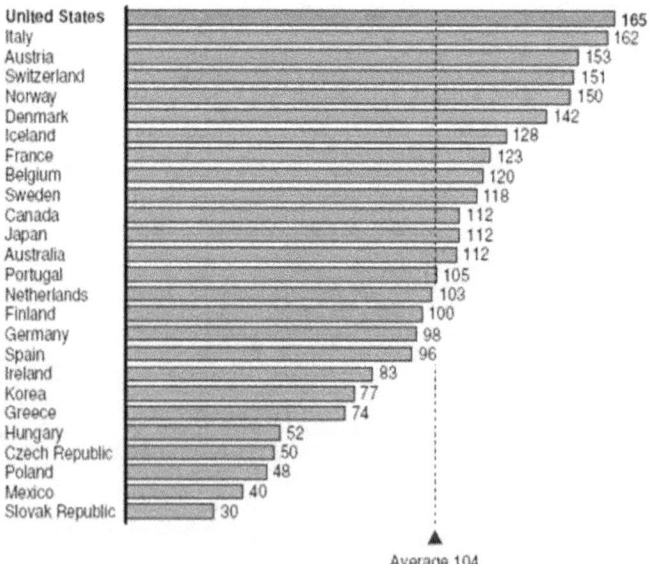

Figure 2.2 Spending On Education by Country

the return on investment is so poor. *The Nation at Risk* report in 1984 could be rewritten today with the same conclusion.

Analyzing this chart makes it clear that a threshold of spending is required. Mexico, for example, only expended $40 per point but their test results are low relative to most countries. However, during the same year, Finland and Canada were two high-performing countries on this international assessment, which spent $100 and $112, respectively. Return on investment in these two countries was considerably higher than what was achieved in the United States.

By 2009, after decades of high spending, American students' scores on the OECD's (PISA) mathematics tests placed the United States in the 26th rank of 65 countries and 11th in reading. Canada, once a strong performer on international assessments, slipped to 5th and 9th respectively, while Mexico ranked 46th and 49th respectively. These PISA tests are given every three years and the *2012 results* demonstrated the following ranks:

- United States: Mathematics at 36th and Reading at 24th
- Canada: Mathematics at 14th and Reading at 6th
- Mexico: Mathematics at 53rd and Reading at 52nd

Pearson, the publishing company, combines results from international tests on cognitive skills with educational attainment in literacy and graduation rates. Their "Learning Curve" provides a global ranking of education systems for 40 OECD countries, which further underscores the relative poor performance by the United States. Americans have a sense of pride in achieving high levels of performance throughout their societal outcomes, but this feeling is not evident in educational outcomes.

In Pearson's 2012 edition of their global rankings, the United States had an overall ranking of 17 out of 40 countries. By 2014, the US ranking improved overall to 14th as a result of recent successes in the cognitive skills component—achieved through *No Child Left Behind*—with an eleventh place ranking. In the Educational Attainment index, the United States ranked 20th overall. If such an American ranking occurred in the Olympics of sport, for example, media would portray these results as catastrophic.

Yet, in education, *mainline media is relatively low key about low levels of performance*, likely because they do not wish to offend the sizable workforce in education. Similar to politicians pandering to educators for voting support, the media pander to their readers and watchers for their support. This is their politically correct response. A high-profile politician in Alberta's Legislature repeatedly said, "It's always about the money." In the media industry, *turning off* subscribers with unwelcome news can result in subscribers *turning away*, leading to lost revenues.

Pearson's methodology provides another version of assessing education systems around the world. Regardless of the system used, the evidence suggests that the United States is well down the ladder on key performance measures of student achievement. National initiatives at educational reform are necessary in order to *ensure that all children receive fair treatment* by participating in educational programs with high standards.

The point is that educational success as measured by international tests has not improved since the 1984 *A Nation at Risk* declaration that the United States suffered from *mediocre educational performance.* Therefore, in this theme of *learning well, living well*, the United States faces risk from both the home and the school contributions in the *circular cause and consequence* discussion.

LAGGING PUBLIC CONFIDENCE

American's *attitudes* toward its education system reveal a *general state of concern.* Notwithstanding that *parents* responding to the 2015 Phi Delta Kappa/Gallup Poll (PDK/Gallup Poll) provide a positive perspective on their child's school, their response is not so glowing when the survey asks, "Students are often given the Grades A, B, C, D, and FAIL to denote the quality of their work. Suppose the public schools themselves in *your community* were graded in the same way. What grade would you give the public schools here—A, B, C, D, or FAIL?"

A response from 51 percent giving A or B is not particularly good news considering that the question dealt with the *local community*. A response of 21 percent giving A or B to the service of schools across the nation is equally disturbing. Educators want to spin these disappointing results by countering with the 72 percent A or B rating for their child's school; however, the disparities evident with the community and national results indicate a need that must be addressed.

When surveys are undertaken, what might be a reasonable response when respondents have a scale of five possible responses? Public sector surveys appear to be more dichotomous (two possible responses) in structure, and relatively few offering five possible responses are available on the internet.

A 2014 national survey in New Zealand on the question of *trust and confidence in police* had the top two of five responses score at 78 percent. A 2015 survey in the United States on the *State Court system being fair and impartial* had 62 percent of respondents scoring that system with a top-two response. Further, a *Huffington Post* US national 2015 survey *about trust in law enforcement* scored 61 percent in the top two responses. From these examples a 51 percent response on the PDK/Gallup Poll for education is not a stellar result.

Canada does not have a system for ongoing monitoring of public opinion concerning education, because it has the least level of federalism in education of any country: a national department of education does not exist. In 2005, the Society for Excellence in Education commissioned a one-time national study that demonstrated a 72 percent top-two response in grading Canada's school system. Again, the PDK/Gallup Poll results for the United States of 51 percent giving a top-two response does not transmit a message of high confidence in American schooling.

In another survey by Ipsos Global @dvisor in 2012, the public responded to the statement, "Most of the money (country) government spends on education is wasted." Americans responded with 39 percent saying "strongly agree" or "tend to agree," and 30 percent of Canadians agreed. A sizable group of taxpayers are disgruntled with their education systems.

Gallup conducts ongoing polling regarding *Confidence in Institutions* about whether respondents have "a great deal" or "quite a lot" of confidence. The June 2015 poll results indicated a score of 31 percent for American public schools. This low result is *not* the vote of confidence educators want!

The Canadian Education Association undertakes periodic reviews of taxpayers' attitudes toward Canada's system of public education. In 2007 they reported a disturbing trend in Canadians' level of confidence in public schools since 1984 when 76 percent of Canadians reported a "great deal" or "fair amount" of confidence. By 2007, public confidence fell a full 31 percentage points to 45 percent. When Canadians responded to the issue of confidence in educational policy, only 19 percent indicated either "great deal" or "quite a lot." These low results in Canada are not a vote of confidence!

CLASS SIZE: WORKING OR LEARNING CONDITION

During recent decades, taxpayers were called upon to fund class size reduction as a major initiative. Teachers, *with their vested interest in workload*, successfully convinced the public that reducing class sizes was the most important aspect necessary for effective teaching. The 2007 *McKinsey Report* (Barber and Mourshed) states,

> Class size reduction has probably been the most widely supported and most extensively funded policy aimed at improving schools. Over the past five years every country in the OECD, except for one, has increased the number of its teachers relative to the number of its students.

Sands (2013) quoting a union official's public statements during negotiations with a provincial government on nonsalary issues, stated, "Teachers understand the provincial government is in a difficult financial situation, but teachers need a deal that addresses their concerns about workload. *I'd remind you that teachers' working conditions are students' learning conditions.*" In a nutshell, this official's words epitomize the understanding that unions want the public to embrace them, and little debate is necessary to demonstrate their success; yet, public attitudes have declined.

As class size reduction strategies gained momentum, a 1999 article by William J. Bennett, a previous US secretary of education, reported that spending on US public education between 1960 and 1995 adjusted for inflation increased by 212 percent. It is not possible to determine how much of this large increase went toward reducing class sizes, but it is safe to conclude that a large portion of it did.

Herein is the myth successfully perpetrated by unions. Their successful effort was to convince the public that class size reduction is a *learning* condition rather than a *working* condition: which is what it really is.

Seldom does the media present in-depth reporting of controversial educational topics. One recent exception to this occurred in Edmonton, Alberta, when the local daily newspaper, the *Edmonton Journal* (2013) published an article by David Staples. He was covering the public release of the 2012 PISA results and their implications for Alberta. He noted that "a coalition of trade unionists, teachers, parents, educators, pundits and opposition parties made it the number one issue in education." His report referenced a TEDTalk by Andreas Schleicher, who manages the PISA international testing program:

> One way you can spend money is by paying teachers well, and you can see Korea investing a lot in attracting the best people into the teaching profession. And Korea also invests into *long school days*, which drives up costs further. Last but not least, Koreans want their teachers not only to teach but also to develop. They invest in professional development and collaboration and many other things. All that costs money. How can Korea afford all of this? The answer is, *students in Korea learn in large classes*. . . . You go to the next country on the list, Luxembourg, and you can see the red dot (representing cost per student) is exactly where it is for Korea, so Luxembourg spends the same per student as Korea does. But, you know, parents and teachers and policymakers in Luxembourg all like small classes. You know, it's very pleasant to walk into a small class. So they have invested all their money into there. . . . *Class size, is driving costs up.* But even Luxembourg can spend its money only once, and the *price for this is that teachers are not paid particularly well.* Students don't have long hours of learning. And basically, teachers have little time to do anything else than teaching. So you can see two countries spent their money very differently, and actually *how they spent their money matters a lot more than how much they invest in education.*

Staples also reported on his personal, follow-up conversation with Schliecher, who added observations regarding the direction Canadian education systems have followed:

> In Canada, a fair amount of its money has been eaten up by reductions in class size. It's been a very expensive move and *you can't reverse it*. Once you've gone that road, nobody is going to accept going back. It's very popular. Teachers like it. Parents like it. It's a very easy to do, very quick to do. But it's a one-way road because nobody is ever going to accept increases in class sizes either. It's very expensive and *it drives out other possibilities.* You can spend your money only once. *If you spend it on a smaller class, you can no longer spend it on more professional development, on better working conditions, or on more pay and so on.*

Schleicher's succinct summary provides politicians across North America with a sobering perspective that cannot be ignored. Disregarding research, while pandering to stakeholders, is costing taxpayers a great deal of money with little to show as a return on investment, but is an entrenched expense almost impossible to reverse. It is also more difficult to alter priorities and move into more productive strategies. *Once launched, initiatives for improved working conditions become entitlements.*

Schleicher's perspective is not anomalous. Barber and Moursed reviewed research from around the world and reported their findings in the 2007 *McKinsey Report*:

> The available evidence suggests that except at the very early grades, class size reduction does not have much impact on student outcomes. Of 112 studies which looked at the impact of the reduction in class sizes on student outcomes, only 9 found any positive relationship, 103 found either no significant relationship, or a significant negative relationship. Even when a significant relationship was found the effect was not substantial.
>
> Most importantly, every single one of the studies showed that within the range of class sizes typical in OECD countries, *variations in teacher quality completely dominate any effect of reduced class size.* At best, reducing class sizes from 23 to 15 students improves achievement by an average student by 8% ile points.

These authors point out that more teachers in the school system require more hiring from the *bottom* of the talent pool. This is counterproductive because *the quality of the education system cannot exceed the quality of its teachers.*

Malcolm Gladwell (2013) provides results from another meta-analysis involving 18 countries. Only two countries—namely Greece and Iceland—experienced a *"non-trivial* benefit in reducing class size." Notably, there was no benefit from reducing class sizes in educational powerhouses such as Japan and Singapore. Yet across the world, countries believe that providing more intimate classrooms will improve student achievement.

In the United States for example, Gladwell reports that 77 percent of the public thinks it makes more sense to lower class sizes than to pay teachers more money. Between 1996 and 2004, approximately 250,000 teachers were added at an increased cost of 21 percent as the United States pursued the teachers' union agenda. Gladwell concludes, "There isn't a single profession in the world that has increased its numbers over the past two decades as much or as quickly or at such expense that teaching has. . . . The evidence suggests that the thing we think is such an advantage might not be an advantage at all."

While exploring this subject, Gladwell provides an interesting perspective on why governments are so "obsessed with what is good about small classes that we have become *oblivious* about what is good about large classes." He postulates that there is a *student critical mass*, and that very low class sizes experience insufficient breadth of opinion.

He provides support for this perspective by referencing Jesse Levin's Dutch study, which determined that the number of peers a student had in the classroom had a surprising correlation to improved academic performance, especially in the case of weaker students. These students felt more normal in larger classes because others in the class were performing in similar ways and asking similar questions. In other words, there is comfort in knowing that classmates are also struggling; this empowers these students, leaving them confident enough to seek additional clarification and help when they encounter a problem.

Similarly, students at the upper end of learning achievement do not wish to have a "nerd" label attached to their name. More classmates likely result in more students with similar capacity engaging in higher-level conversations. There is comfort in knowing that others in the class are similarly inclined, and there is value to weaker students in hearing the discussion modeled by stronger peers.

Gladwell summarizes his research on class size with two important observations. *First, children are not only competitors for teacher attention but also allies in the adventure of learning.* This observation appears to be a response to the many educators who complain that more students in the class reduce the time educators can spend with each student. In other words, *student learning is facilitated not only by the teacher but also by peers.*

This second observation undercuts the argument private schools often make to justify their high tuition fees. According to them, their low class sizes ensure students will do better. They also make the most of the myth that spending a lot of money solves problems. In other words, buying more teachers to reduce class sizes will *always* produce better learning. *This argument has convinced a lot of parents but its basic premise is doubtful at best and they should be wary of this marketing strategy.*

Challenging a myth is one purpose of this chapter. Confidence in public education is waning because *learning well is too focused on inputs.* Special interests combined with political motivation are focused inappropriately and are driving up costs without appropriate returns in what really matters: educational outcomes. *Success in learning well is necessary for living well. A significant error has been to consider class size as a learning well issue.*

When governments promote measuring and reporting on inputs, such as class size, they communicate to the public that inputs matter, and evaluation on these inputs should be the focus for accountability. Politically correct thinking places teachers rather than students atop the pyramid. This perspective must change! The next chapter explains how such a change can be achieved so that improvement occurs.

KEY POINTS

- Learning well is the product of an interplay between the home and the school, and the data story for the education system regarding success in achieving its mandate for learning well is cause for concern.
- Teachers' unions have been successful in their negotiations but are seen as a stumbling block for educational reform.
- The high percentage of educators in our workforce places considerable pressure on politicians to reduce expectations by yielding to teachers' demands during negotiations.
- Despite high levels of spending, American students' performance on international tests clearly demonstrate that the United States is at risk.
- Mainline media is relatively low key about low levels of performance: likely because they do not wish to offend the education's sizable workforce.
- Reducing class size is more appropriately classified as a working than a learning condition.

Chapter 3

Moving from Intuition to Intelligence

The previous chapter reviewed the *circular cause and consequence* issue regarding a slogan, *learning well, living well*. Effective development of students' *cognitive abilities* benefits from a school system supplemented with strong support from the home. International assessments document consistently poor results in the United States and now declining results in Canada relative to other countries in the world. Public confidence in our school system reflects a concern that, despite significant spending, *expectations are not being achieved.*

Teachers and their union representatives successfully convinced our political leaders that spending in education is an appropriate measure of government performance. This mistaken belief is most evident in the education system's success in promoting class size as a *learning condition* rather than a *working condition*, despite a lack of evidence that their contention is factual. The rationale applied by decision-makers is based more on *intuition than on intelligence. Emotions* rather than *empirical* evidence play too large a role in educational decisions.

Focusing on emotions benefits special interests because isolated stories are powerful tools for turning public opinion. Media also find it more convenient to retell the story than research factual information unless it is provided which, in education, would have to come from *administrators or politicians*. These groups understand that a politically correct activity is to lie low and stay out of the unions' line of fire so that they do not become a target.

Effective decision making in the education system is hindered by the political reality that teachers represent a significant percentage of voters. Pandering for votes plays an important role in the democratic process because governments are inclined to accommodate the wishes of special interests more than what is in the best interests of the country, state, or province. Leadership is key to providing students with an effective education and the school system is unfair to students when their best interests are compromised by governments paying greater heed to intuition driven by emotion than intelligence determined by data. *Changing this culture is the focus of this chapter.*

CHILDREN ARE MORE ACCOUNTABLE THAN GOVERNMENTS

Accountability and transparency became public sector buzzwords in the early 1990s; yet, governments are making slow progress toward its implementation. Governments are not unlike the general population. Both tend to resist efforts to be held accountable or to make public any information regarding their performance; yet, they *enthusiastically proclaim their desire to hold others accountable.* Governments, for example, focus attention on holding corporations accountable while refusing to expose their own leadership to similar levels of scrutiny.

The private sector excluded, few people working in the public sector surpass the accountability required of a Grade 1 student. Indeed, it is a moral dilemma that our children are held to higher degrees of accountability than most public sector workers as well as all governments. Herein is the *shame* and *sham* of our democratic institutions.

Consider that each student receives a *written formal evaluation* on his work approximately 50 times before graduating twelve years later. His performance will be *rated* (symbols/letter grades) and *ranked* (percent/letter grades) in multiple subjects (reading/math/etc.) and in multiple areas within each subject. Occasionally a "failing" assessment occurs unless the school is still devoted to the now ill-regarded practice of social promotion.

Politicians, on the other hand, indicate that their accountability is every *four years* when elections are held. During the twelve years when our children attend school, governments are held accountable on approximately three occasions, and the decision is likely based more on emotional reasons than on empirical data. Significant emphasis is placed on candidates' capacity to debate when "one-line zingers" grab media attention and too frequently lead to "winner" declarations.

DECLINING PUBLIC TRUST IN GOVERNMENT

When we value our children so much that they, as students, are held to such high standards of accountability, it is logical to expect that governments be held to at least similar, if not greater, levels of accountability. The public's frustration with government is evident in Gallup polling through their schedule of surveying public confidence in institutions. The 2015 poll revealed the lowest level of confidence in institutions for the US Congress with 8 percent of respondents indicating "great deal" or "quite a lot" of confidence.

This high level of dissatisfaction dominated the 2016 presidential election when candidates resorted to foul language and name calling. Nasty exchanges between candidates captivated public attention because anger against the political establishment prevailed. Voters recalled the 1976 film *Network*, which was famous for the sentence, "I'm as mad as hell and I won't take it anymore." Broken promises, political gridlock, and uncontrollable spending were some of the issues fueling public anger and legitimizing unpresidential behavior.

While many factors conspired to diminish trust in government performance, including the school system, there is also the reality that loss of trust in government services is a global trend. *In short, if the government is involved there is a likelihood of public mistrust.* A presentation on June 3, 2009, by Globescan to a group of government officials demonstrates how seriously trust in the government has declined. In 1964, Globescan reported that 77 percent of the American public indicated they trusted the government. By 1980 only 26 percent admitted this. While trust rose to 43 percent in 1984, it bounced between 20 percent and 30 percent since 1990 and 2006.

There is merit in providing greater context for this loss of trust. Globescan conducted four surveys between 2001 and 2005 in fourteen countries—Argentina, Canada, France, Germany, Great Britain, India, Indonesia, Italy, Mexico, Nigeria, Russia, Spain, Turkey, and the United States. It obtained a net rating of averages across these countries by subtracting nontrust from trust and comparing the result with other significant groups. The net ratings are as follows:

- nongovernmental organizations (+29);
- United Nations (+13);
- large local companies (+2);
- *national governments (−9);* and
- global companies (−15).

By 2006, North American trust levels had a dramatically negative impact on the average for the group of fourteen countries. With only approximately 30 percent of citizens in both Canada and the United States reporting "trust" in the government, the net rating was at approximately a minus forty level. *The North American average for distrust of its government is a serious issue as we watch politicians borrow money today so that they have a better chance of being elected tomorrow.* Then, at some future time, they retire, leaving their citizenry, more specifically the children, to deal with the debts incurred by their reelection efforts. Bluntly stated, *this is failing leadership that is producing an unconscionable situation.*

MOVE AWAY FROM INPUTS TOWARD OUTCOMES

Improvement in confidence and trust in government necessitates a change in perspective. The public is predisposed to measuring inputs where judgments regarding quality are based on the amount of *funding* invested in programs and services. Governments are to blame for this perspective because their response to any problem in our society generally includes a commitment to throw more money at it. Funding levels are readily measured and compared. Therefore, the public is conditioned to the notion that *spending more will achieve more. People frequently confuse activity with effectiveness* because they think that the act of doing something will improve the situation *automatically.*

Once a program is in place the law of inertia sets in and it continues because it is difficult for political leadership to retreat from commitments, and people in those programs can put government officials in a defensive position when contemplating eliminating their coveted program. For example, educators can quickly rally a parent group to complain vociferously when a funding cut is projected to a program enrolling their child. People are still persuaded by the subjective anecdotal evidence the educators provide even though it is recognized that the teachers had a great deal of time invested in the program and their jobs were likely threatened in the event legislators reduced funding.

When a school applies for and receives special funding for a new program, parents are easily persuaded about the program's virtue when their child is identified for placement. Evaluations of these programs usually lack rigor associated with empirical data based on student outcomes; rather, qualitative assessments are utilized focusing on *attitudes* about being in the program. Considerations to remove funding for the program are countered with strong opposition generated by parents with children who receive the special attention.

What is always interesting about these instances is that the school or, for that matter, the district, *appears to place little value on the efficacy of these programs.* There is excitement in launching a new venture but not in conducting a tedious effort to evaluate the outcomes. Experience has shown that assessments are usually based on survey results focused on *qualitative* rather than *quantitative* evaluation. Respondents, typically teachers and parents, are biased because parents like the special attention their child is receiving and teachers either like the fact that they can pursue their passion or that the program has removed a particular problem from their workload.

If it is determined that an initiative truly has value in terms of improving outcomes, it is logical to expect that a school would retain the program and find funding by withdrawing resources from other programs where "bang for the buck" is less. This exchange seldom happens, however. The emotional pain associated with ending a program and deploying those resources toward a more promising venture seems too great.

More broadly speaking, the problem is that governments implement new initiatives resulting in added cost to taxpayers but they seldom evaluate worthiness to determine whether programs should continue. When the next need is determined, they resort, once again, to their predisposition to throw money at problems. *Funding is seldom found from within the system but is merely added, and so the bill to taxpayers keeps increasing.* Soon a smorgasbord of initiatives is operating in the system, which prevents the measurement of any particular program's worthiness.

This can be illustrated by a Canadian provincial government, which increased its annual operational funding to the education system by 112 percent over a fourteen-year period. During this same time period, inflation only increased by 47 percent and student population increased by 9 percent. Funding the original set of *needs*—inflation and growth—fourteen years later required an additional 56 percent. Coincidentally, the *expansionary budget* necessary to fund newly identified *wants* was also 56 percent. During this fourteen-year period, government added an average of *4 percent annual spending beyond inflation and growth for newly identified initiatives.*

These additional expenditures included efforts to decrease class sizes across all grade levels but especially in primary grades. This effort was supplemented by an initiative to improve reading achievement among primary children. Even though these initiatives were focused primarily on children in the primary grades, class sizes in high school courses were also reduced considerably.

Additional funding was allocated for dealing with increased numbers of children identified as possessing mild to moderate disability. This latter increase was ironical because an audit of this category revealed 50 percent of students identified by school personnel did not meet the criterion. Removing the annual audit process resulted in fraudulent behavior with a dramatic increase in the number of students identified as having special needs because schools recognized that the government had created a "cash cow" that they could milk.

Another significant grant was given to the system for exploring new ideas. Innovation should be encouraged and when it is, there is invariably a need for additional resources. The question is whether innovation strategies should be evaluated to determine their contribution to improved student outcomes. *It seems self-evident that empirical evidence should demonstrate an agreed upon return within a reasonable period of time.*

An analysis of assessments undertaken in this initiative demonstrated a lack of *empirical* data with inordinate use of satisfaction surveys. Commitments to evaluate improved student achievement were conspicuously absent but programs were operational and, once implemented, removing them was virtually impossible. This is a common situation facing government programs, and is a significant reason for an increasing public sector debt.

Interestingly, the salaries of educators increased significantly during this same fourteen-year period. As already stated, inflation increased by 47 percent during these years but salaries increased by 60 percent or almost 1 percent *beyond* the annual inflation rate. Data revealed that educators' salaries in the province increased more than double that of another province with the next highest increase. Political leaders from other provinces expressed their concern that this one province was needlessly driving up the cost of education across the country; this had a knock-on effect that compelled governments elsewhere to increase their teacher salaries beyond what they deemed to be reasonable.

Unfortunately, the substantial increase in financial input did not result in a corresponding increase in student achievement. This region's performance on national and international assessments demonstrated a steady decline in reading and mathematics scores to the extent that ongoing visitations from other regions wanting to learn from previous levels of success virtually ended. Innovative international educators reacted predictably by voting with their feet: they knew that achievement was waning in spite of government funding increases and they wanted to move to areas of the world where *student achievement remained the paramount concern.*

Perhaps an even more telling indicator of the decline occurred when the testing agency released the PISA international comparative test scores. Rather than follow the government's traditional practice of holding a press conference to publicly celebrate success, they quietly released the disappointing results on a government website. *Embarrassment and lack of transparency became the new norms.*

Meanwhile, educators in this jurisdiction were happy with the class size reductions because it meant more jobs, which provided them with more career options. Unions were happy because more educators in the system meant more union dues. Administrators were happy because more teachers meant higher administrative allowances. Parents were happy because they believed their children were the recipient of special focus and attention. The public was happy because the government was spending more money on their community.

The culmination of all of this happiness was that politicians were happy because everyone else was happy and the prospect of reelection improved. The only fly in the ointment was *that achievement was decreasing and few knew, and even fewer were upset enough to protest or take action.*

PUBLIC WILLINGNESS TO SPENDING IS SHIFTING

At some point the financial impact becomes burdensome to the degree that there is an implosion. In the United States, faced with a huge and growing deficit, the PDK/Gallup Poll asked the American public which was more important for the federal government to do in the next five years—balance the federal budget or improve the quality of the education system in the nation? *A dramatic shift in public opinion occurred during a sixteen-year period with only 25 percent indicating "balancing the federal budget" in 1996 but 60 percent in 2012.*

Overspending is a serious problem in many countries. A sampling of countries at the beginning of 2016 on NationalDebtClocks.org demonstrates how governments are operating beyond their budgets thereby incurring approximate *per person (including babies) indebtedness* (in US dollars):

- *Canada at $23,000*
- Russia at $1,700
- *United States at $58,000*
- China at $4,000
- United Kingdom at $36,000
- India at $800
- Germany at $28,000
- South Korea at $10,000
- France at $35,000
- *Greece at $38,000*

These examples demonstrate the perilous degree to which countries spend beyond their means. Noteworthy is Greece's indebtedness relative to other countries after the worldwide attention focused on its financial status within the Eurozone. Indebtedness is a particularly troublesome issue because governments appear incapable of making cuts to accommodate new initiatives. *Politicians are careless with other peoples' money.*

In a culture where inputs are examined more readily than outcomes, governments allocate new funds for any initiative believed to hold increased promise for students. Class size is a prime example where governments spend on "hope" rather than on "facts." When our misguided politicians become frustrated with poor results from such programs they approved, they look for other solutions that will, hopefully, "trump" the failure.

Eventually the smorgasbord of programs reaches an impasse: *they are too costly to maintain, while at the same time they are too engrained in society to be discontinued.* The result is financial paralysis, which is a situation that is readily apparent in many European and North American countries.

The point is that public sector organizations, such as the education system, have limitless wants, which require higher levels of funding. Many governments are tiring of these never-ending requests and want to see improved results. At the same time, a business model that envisions balanced budgets, appropriate returns on investment, and accountability is finding its way into the public sector.

Educators are reacting with alarm to the monitoring of outcomes and the prospect of consequences for failed performance. If the new approach is adopted it will be less likely to blame "them"—the government—for shortcomings; instead, the finger of accountability will be pointed at "us" the teacher, the union, and the school.

A NEW WAY OF THINKING

The ill-fated practice of adding programs and services without eliminating poor-performing ones is creating financial risk for countries and their citizens. A new way of thinking is required so that government programs, such as education, are accountable. *Accountability without consequences is not accountability!* While consequences can be both *positive* and *negative*, there must be program casualties when outcomes are not improving. Governing on the basis of emotion must be replaced by making decisions on the basis of evidence.

The Preneurcast website outlines how removing emotion from decision making can occur through Zero Based Thinking (ZBT). The analogy to describe this simple concept is to think through the approaches a stockholder would take if he or she sold all stocks every day and then, without brokerage fees, bought the next. It is unlikely that the same stocks would be purchased the next day because we would recognize the futility of chasing a loss knowing *that loss is killing your gains.*

"Spinning on a dime" is easier in the business environment where information on outcomes flows more readily. The government's information-gathering process requires a longer cycle and public sector enterprises, such as education, require spinning on a coin the size of a dollar. Nevertheless, ZBT is still applicable in the public sector's annual budget cycle.

Instituting accountability approaches such as ZBT in education requires a measurement process not unlike that which is used with students in the school system. The time has come when the education system is held to standards of accountability equal to, if not greater, than how it holds its students accountable. Outlined below are the essential aspects of an accountability program for education that can be used to evaluate and report on progress:

TIME FRAME: Students receive a summative evaluation annually with progress reviews throughout the year. Similarly, the school system will benefit from an annual report card that accommodates more frequent updating as new information is available.

DUAL EVALUATION: Student evaluations provide an assessment comparing both *achievement* for the grade—also known as standards—and *improvement* relative to previous performance. School system evaluations must also address both components:

Standards/Achievement: One method is to identify similar regions and calculate the average level of performance to determine a baseline for each measure. A second method is to measure current performance for each measure and then "freeze" that level of performance as a baseline for evaluating future performance. Establishing cut points above and below these baselines provides the basis for evaluating future performance relative to standards. Over a considerable time period or in the event of a significant change in demographic factors, adjustments may be required to reflect new realities.

The achievement evaluation compares the current school system result against fixed standards for each measure. The cut points could be set by selecting the 5th, 25th, 75th, and 95th percentiles on the distribution of baseline scores. The comparison of the current result to the standards results in one of the following achievement levels: • very high for results at or above the 95th percentile; • high for results between the 75th and 95th percentiles; • intermediate for results between the 25th and 75th percentiles; • low for results between the 5th and 25th percentiles, and • very low for results below the 5th percentile.

Improvement: This approach considers *comparisons with self*. When student achievement is assessed, it is important to address performance relative to standards or expectations, but it is equally important to assess improvement in the context of previous assessments. In this approach the improvement evaluation compares the current school system result with prior three-year average results for each measure, using a statistical test to determine the extent of change. This results in one of the following improvement levels: • improved significantly; • improved, • maintained, • declined, and • declined significantly.

The evaluations of achievement and improvement can then be combined for an overall evaluation for the measure, resulting in one of the following: • excellent, • good, • acceptable, • issue, and • concern.

Critical to understanding these methodologies is a review regarding what once was a common, but a fundamentally inappropriate approach. Initial approaches in assessing performance focused on comparisons with all school systems regardless of whether they served advantaged or disadvantaged communities. Educators understood the relationship between the home and school environments, and strongly objected to comparisons where these differences were not neutralized. The preceding approach emphasizing dual evaluation overcomes that wrong-minded approach because comparisons involve a meaningful and defensible standard as well as previous levels of performance.

MULTIPLE RATINGS

The education system recognizes the value of using multiple ratings, such as letter grades, symbols, and percentages, when assessing student achievement. Students experience greater motivation from feedback using multiple levels than that which occurs when their work is assessed using the pass/fail model. Parents have a greater understanding of their child's strengths and weaknesses when achievement is rated using a multiple system of codes.

A report card for a school system should include a scoring system involving a minimum of five ratings. The illustration above utilizes an evaluation for achievement based on the terms excellent, good, acceptable, issue, and concern. For the improvement component, usable terms could be improved significantly, improved, maintained, declined, and declined significantly.

A method for improving understanding of these ratings is to provide visual enhancement through color. For example, the five-point rating scales used above can be achieved using the colors blue, green, yellow, orange, and red. Such an enhancement makes the reporting instrument more user friendly because overall performance is readily discerned through the eye gate.

MULTIPLE CRITERIA

Just as students receive evaluations of their achievement for different subjects, school systems' evaluations should assess performance in multiple areas and, where necessary, from multiple sources—for example, students, teachers, parents, etc. These multiple areas include:

Safe and Caring: Percentages of teachers, parents, and students who agree that students are safe at school, are learning the importance of caring and respect for others, and are treated fairly in school. For example, teachers, parents, and students are asked: whether students feel safe at school and safe on the way to and from school, whether they treat each other well at school, whether teachers care about their students, and whether students are treated fairly by adults at school.

Program of Studies: Percentages of teachers, parents, and students satisfied with the opportunity for students to receive a broad program of studies, including fine arts, career, technology, health, and physical education. For example, teachers, parents, and students are asked about the variety of courses available to students at school and the opportunities they have at school to: learn music, drama, art, computers, health, another language, or participate in physical education.

Education Quality: Percentages of teachers, parents, and students satisfied with the overall quality of basic education. For example, teachers, parents, and students are asked about the following: the overall quality of education in the child's school, the quality of teaching in school, what is being learned in the core subjects that is useful (students), whether students are learning what they need to know (parents and teachers), whether school work is interesting and challenging, and whether learning expectations at school are clear.

Satisfaction with Program Access: Percentages of teachers, parents, and students satisfied with the accessibility, effectiveness, and efficiency of programs and services for students in their community. For example, teachers, parents, and students are asked about the following services for students in schools: academic counseling, career counselling, library services, and support for students with special needs.

Dropout Rate: Annual dropout rate of students aged 14 to 18.

High School Completion Rate (3 years): Percentages of students who completed high school within three years of entering Grade 10. The 3 rather than 4-year rate is chosen because it communicates a commitment to efficiency.

Student Achievement: Test results for each group and subject assessed.

Postsecondary Transition Rate (6 years): Percentages of students who have enrolled in a postsecondary program within six years of entering Grade 10.

Scholarship Eligibility Rate: Percentages of Grade 12 students who meet the scholarship eligibility criteria.

Preparation for Lifelong Learning: Percentages of teachers and parents satisfied that high school graduates demonstrate the knowledge, skills, and attitudes necessary for lifelong learning. For example, teachers and parents are asked whether their children/high school students are taught, and demonstrate, the knowledge, skills, and attitudes necessary for learning throughout their lifetimes.

Work Preparation: Percentages of teachers and parents who agree that students are taught attitudes and behaviors that will make them successful at work when they finish school. For example, teachers and parents are asked to indicate whether their children/students are taught attitudes and behaviors that will enable them to be successful at work when they leave school.

Citizenship: Percentages of teachers, parents, and students who are satisfied that students model the characteristics of active citizenship. For example, teachers, parents, and students are asked whether they/their children/students: help each other, respect each other, follow the rules, and are encouraged at school to try their best and be involved in activities that help the community.

Parental Involvement: Percentages of teachers and parents satisfied with parental involvement in decisions about their child's education. For example, teachers and parents are asked: about the opportunity for parental involvement in decisions about their child's education, the opportunity for parental involvement in decisions at their child's school, whether parental input into decisions at their child's school is considered, and whether parents are involved "a lot" or "a little" with decisions about their child's education.

School Improvement: Percentages of teachers, parents, and students indicating that their school and schools in their jurisdiction have improved or stayed the same the last three years. For example, teachers and parents are asked whether the quality of education at the school where their children studied has improved, stayed the same, or declined in the past three years. Students are asked whether they are proud of their school and whether they would recommend it to a friend.

GRADE LEVEL OF ACHIEVEMENT MEASURE

One additional significant measure is to have teachers record each student's year-end, *grade level of achievement* (GLA) in *reading* and *mathematics*. From personal experience, this type of assessment is not an onerous task as the question has been posed, not only at year-end but at every reporting period, to hundreds of teachers on thousands of students. Every teacher can respond to the question, "Is this student 'at', 'above' or 'below' their grade placement?" GLA brings the teacher's assessment of student achievement into the suite of hard data measures where test scores now prevail.

Seasoned teacher evaluators will immediately recognize a weakness in using GLA as a measure for assessing teacher performance. Grade inflation is a serious problem when teachers assess their own students, and incorporating GLA into performance evaluations encourages teachers to inflate results for their own benefit. Recording this information on the report card serves to reduce an educational concern identified as "standards creep."

Experience reveals that this concern is overcome when the response to the GLA question is recorded several times a year. Patterns are readily discerned when students move into different classes at year-end and the question is posed to receiving teachers. Integrity in this process is achieved when the principal monitors the teachers' evaluations in subsequent years. Not only is this measurement a check and balance to inflated assessments in the classroom but it can also be incorporated into the accountability framework.

ACCOUNTABILITY WITHOUT CONSEQUENCES IS NOT ACCOUNTABILITY

It is essential that reporting on students in their place of work be balanced in order that the focus will be on their *achievement* as well as *improvement*. All aspects of their work, including effort, can assist parents in their understanding of how well their child is succeeding. Reporting on school system performance that utilizes a balanced scorecard enhances accountability and transparency, and staff as well as the public can determine progress and areas where greater effort is required. The model outlined above is one representation of many possibilities, but it provides a starting point when looking to achieve an *accountable* and *transparent* organization.

Skeptics of the immense value of a school and district report card need only spend a few minutes observing shoppers in the aisles of grocery stores. A quick trip down these aisles is replaced with extensive examination of ingredients now that these are displayed on wrappings. Shoppers are aware of this feature and their scrutiny of the information portends the degree to which parents will pay heed to school level accountability reports.

Instituting an accountability framework requires decisions regarding poor performance. Making these decisions is when the "rubber meets the road" because accountability requires *consequences* or it simply is not accountability. In other words, *counting is not accounting!* Outlining these consequences at the launch of a system report card is better than attempting to develop them when a response to poor performance is "staring in the face" of one or more of the organizations.

In Alberta, for example, student achievement on provincial tests was a primary issue and necessitated government response when school district results were in decline. Steps initiating progressive discipline were hotly contested within the government's bureaucracy because applying consequences was seen as wielding a "negative stick." This politically correct concern engendered considerable support; however, agreement emerged that the *correct position was to place students atop the pyramidal pinnacle*. Applying consequences to declining student achievement was necessary leadership.

In this instance, three of the 62 school districts experienced two consecutive "significantly declined" evaluations on their annual report card for student achievement. Improvement, or lack thereof, is an important component of this evaluation program and these consecutive declines at the significant level triggered *prescribed consequences*. Step one was to issue a "letter of warning" indicating that these districts were on watch and that "failure to improve will result in further actions."

These further actions were not spelled out in the letter but school districts knew that the School Act articulated three consequences that the government could employ. One was to launch a public investigation so that the community would acquire greater understanding of the problem. The remaining two had been used previously for financial imprudence but *never for failure to achieve student success*. Specifically, the superintendent's contract might not be renewed or the school board would be replaced with an official trustee.

Initiating this progressive discipline produced immediate and astonishing results. In one school district, student achievement merited "significantly improved" for each of the next two years. In the other two districts, the results improved in year one and merited "improved significantly" in year two with achievement rates at their highest recorded levels. *There is a clear and important role that provinces and states play, and that is ignored by those who think that once the system gives all power to the principal or superintendent, then there is no meaningful role for any other leadership level.*

Two years later, a different school board earned the dubious distinction of being replaced on the *basis of overwhelmingly poor student outcomes*. Previously, such dramatic action was only precipitated by financial imprudence or dysfunctional behavior in the boardroom. Firing a school board based on harming student learning had never been politically correct.

Everyone working in the education system has their rights formally protected by contracts, government legislation, and school district policies. Students, the clients of our school system, do not have their educational rights protected in such formal ways. Accountability mechanisms, which instruct the system about what is important and how well outcomes are being achieved, are a way to codify students' rights.

Fullan (2005) stated leadership's mandate succinctly: "System level leaders have a moral obligation to intervene *explicitly and directly* in cases where schools are failing children." Children only receive *one chance* at their education and school systems are responsible to get it right for them. *Failure is not an option!* There are occasions when we learn a leadership principle that *all governments make a difference* but *outcomes* determine whether it is *positive* or *negative*.

Moving from *intuition to intelligence* is the important issue which, in the public sector including education, is given too little credence. Public organizations now employ public relations personnel whose task is to communicate positive messages about their organization. These "spinners" endeavor to get messages out before the media can deliver its interpretation, which may be less favorable. Evaluations on a report card take the spin out from the spinners.

One provincial premier ventured into the development of a provincial report card without being fully aware of its implications. When bureaucrats across all departments neared completion of the mandate, they were confronted by the government's "chief spinner" with the question, "Does this then mean that the public can use this document to evaluate government?" The affirmative response immediately produced a *cease and desist order* from the premier. It is one thing to release data in a *score card*, but when the information is also *rated or evaluated* as in a *report card*, power is transferred to citizens.

"Spinners" soon become job hunters when the public has access to performance *assessments* vetted through a public process. When rules in building these assessments are open and consistently applied, "spinners" are no longer necessary to provide the interpretation, and this increased *transparency* promotes a higher level of democracy. A properly constructed report card provides the public with a consistent assessment of services governments provide and, in the process, make hired spinners redundant. Transparency breeds higher levels of public trust.

There are implications to the media as well because "media spinners" were deemed necessary to dig deeper to counter governments' proclivity for "cherry picking" and releasing only positive messaging. These media spinners thrive on creating controversy and also want to avoid consistent assessments so that they can *spin their interpretation* of governments' performance.

Report cards, such as the one described earlier, empower the public's ability to assess performance and provide less credence to the media's intent to invent conflict by focusing merely on the negative. A well-balanced report card reveals the *good, bad, and ugly* for everyone to see, and can be a force to encourage the media to delve deeper into issues. Again, the public wins.

The point is that education's governance—state or province, school districts, and schools—must embrace accountability and transparency by providing public access to ratings of performance relative to student outcomes. One of many potential models is described in this chapter; however, models must first and foremost meet the test of holding service providers more accountable than what we require of a Grade 1 child.

KEY POINTS

- Emotions rather than empirical evidence play too large a role in educational decisions.
- It is a moral dilemma that our children are held to higher degrees of accountability than most public sector workers as well as all governments.

- If the government is involved there is a likelihood of public mistrust.
- A predisposition to measure inputs should be replaced with a report card that evaluates progress on student outcomes.
- Government spending worldwide is resulting in massive public debt.
- Public attitudes toward deficit spending are shifting toward more controlled spending.
- A detailed model for holding the education system is provided.
- Responsible governments demonstrate accountability when they apply consequences for consistently poor performance.

Chapter 4

Harnessing Power through Comparability

The private sector understands comparability. In fact, everyone does and everyone benefits from it. Our economic system is built around the concept that people *want to have choices* where they shop and which product of many similar ones they will purchase. Our market economy is based on supply and demand with little or no government control, and buyers and sellers are allowed to transact freely based on a mutually agreed upon price.

Principles involved in our financial dealings are so engrained that we take them for granted, and act in dramatic fashion when opportunities to take advantage of choice are presented. People sensing a "great deal" will line up and even "camp out" overnight in order to *have the best choice*. Black Friday in the United States and Boxing Day in Canada epitomize people's overwhelming interest in principles related to comparability. These specific events are the quintessential moments when comparability motivates peoples' behaviors; yet, the same principles are evident daily whether we purchase gasoline, cars, shoes, groceries, clothing, televisions, smart phones, or houses.

Our currency is the common element for comparing products and services. When participating in cross-border shopping, Americans and Canadians know what their respective dollars are worth and are mindful of differing values in exchange rates. Citizens within each country understand the value of their dollar when crossing state borders in the United States or provincial boundaries in Canada. Taxes may vary across regions within a country but currency does not. Crossing national borders is entirely different and seldom is the dollar of equal value in both countries.

Chapter 4

COMPARABILITY RESISTED IN EDUCATION

An attitudinal shift occurs when we examine comparability principles in the public sector, specifically in education. Herein is a *great divide* where value for money spent is ignored, comparability in quality of service is relatively inconsequential, and low expectations in performance are tolerated. *Competition is openly discouraged!* Comparability between regions lacks transparency.

Workers in the education sector vilify efforts toward comparability because they focus more on self than on students, but are successful in persuading the public that their pursuit of self-interest benefits students. Politicians pander for votes from this special interest and become *complicit in their deceptions.* Such is the political power that comes with being a nation's largest workforce.

The previous chapter is devoted to a need for the education system to construct a measuring and reporting tool known as a balanced scorecard and to use this tool as a report card. This approach is necessary for changing the public's focus on outcomes rather than inputs, increasing accountability and transparency within the school system, and bolstering public trust by being more open.

These report cards can operate at any level whether it be at the school, school district, state/province, or national levels. They provide constituents with a *consistent rating* of performance and ensure a level of accountability and transparency for generating *a winning environment.* The significant aspect is to move beyond merely "cherry-picking" results, which leaders can spin for their benefit, to a process that *reports and evaluates* in a standardized manner on a broad range of *outcomes.* Educators evaluate student performance in their work and it is logical that we similarly assess the performance of our school system.

Providing a comprehensive report on performance is essential and building comparability across the largest geographical region possible strengthens accountability and transparency. Comparability is a matter that separates the private from the public sector. In the former, people demonstrate comparability when they choose a product or service presumably on the basis of best price and/or best service. It would be an act of folly for a government to decree that customers patronize a specific store; yet, *unfettered choice is not a feature within our public school system.* This issue will be addressed in more detail in the next chapter.

When report cards on our schools are implemented, debate on consistency and comparability naturally follows. The pattern evident in student reporting should provide direction for how we report on school performance. Generally speaking, teachers are not permitted to devise their own reporting system for their classroom. They may add supplementary material but schools adopt a school-wide reporting format. Many school districts adopt a similar perspective by requiring the same reporting practices across all schools within the district. In some instances, common report cards are implemented across the entire state or province.

The point is that the public, especially parents, want information reported in a consistent manner to prevent confusion and misunderstanding. They want to *compare* how their child is succeeding from one year to the next as well as how that progress *compares* with standards or expectations. Consistency in reporting is an important issue in a society where families are considerably more mobile than previously.

One Canadian principal in Calgary during the 1980s explained a natural process undertaken whenever a student moved to his school from the province of Ontario. That province did not have curriculum standards identified and did not use any form of standardized assessment. Whenever students arrived from Ontario, this principal counseled with parents on a strategy to uphold the children's feelings of self-worth.

Rather than automatically place the new student in the same grade as in Ontario, the approach was to place this student back one year. It was easier on the student to be moved forward if the instructional program was too easy than to make the shift back because the child found the placement too difficult. A meeting involving school staff with the child's parents was convened shortly thereafter to review the evidence. In only a *few* instances were students moved forward even though *the final decision rested with the parents.*

Grade inflation in these Ontario students' previous setting was so high and grade standards so low that these students would have experienced too much frustration in working with peers who were so far advanced. Years later, Ontario revamped its curriculum and instituted standardized testing which produced significantly improved educational outcomes in student achievement. The 1980s approach is no longer necessary.

This principal in Calgary refused to incorporate a trend toward social promotion choosing, instead, to require that students achieve grade-level standards. The school served an extremely disadvantaged community: telephone booths were installed to compensate for the many homes unable to afford a telephone. Yet, comparisons with other schools in Calgary revealed that student achievement exceeded expectations to such a high degree that the superintendent requested a meeting at the school for the purpose of reviewing what might be applied to the other *200 schools* in the district.

CONSTITUTIONAL LIMITATIONS

Comparing performance on educational indicators faces a significant roadblock. Report cards assessing school performance using a variety of indicators is becoming more common *within* a number of US states and Canadian provinces. However, these two countries also share a common constitutional provision where education is *not* within the mandate of the federal government: a provision significantly limiting comparability.

Lurie (2013) perceives this absence of constitutional authority for the federal government as a significant weakness. His analysis of constitutions worldwide is that 174—almost every country other than the United States and Canada—provide for a "constitutional guarantee to education." Omitting references to education appears to then *promote territorialism among the states and provinces* whereby any pursuit of "common" requires negotiation and consent. *Efforts to reform are splintered, which may not be in the best interests of the entire country.* Nevertheless, it is what it is, and North American education is a mandate owned by the state or province.

It is noteworthy, however, that access to comparable assessments on school performance is evident *within* numerous states and provinces. Such assessments are limited to regions that do *not* cross state or provincial boundaries, which then provide opportunity for citizens within a region to compare with outcomes in others. Capacity for comparing assessment consistently applied across these state or provincial boundaries is not welcomed by the politicians of these regions.

Comparability is gaining support but a significant hurdle remains because substantial regional differences are evident in both countries. These differences in the quality of performance are tolerated because governments lack courage to reveal the outcomes of their leadership—especially when it is failing. *All leadership makes a difference. At issue is whether that difference is positive or negative.*

In Canada, a meeting of high-ranking education bureaucrats from each province was discussing the development of a *common curriculum* across the country. This approach would save money because each province would not be duplicating work in curriculum development, and it would raise standards across the nation because expected outcomes would be those of the highest performing province: perhaps even higher. A common curriculum still allowed for unique needs in social studies where a focus on local regions is necessary.

Students across Canada would benefit from pursuing high standards enhancing the potential for *learning well, living well*. In a country without a federal office for education—the only one in the world—such cooperation would be exceptional! Cooperation between provincial governments in education could set an example for pursuing other efforts at achieving objectives related to the nation's well-being.

This discussion of a common curriculum was quickly chilled because senior officials realized there was potential then for *common assessment*. *Comparability was a frightening possibility* for most of these representatives who claimed that their governments would be worried about overwhelmingly negative reaction from their teachers' unions. Rather than duplicate expenditures on test development within each region, one assessment could be utilized across the country. Financial savings would further mute the teachers' union's criticism about funding being spent provincially on accountability.

The academically weakest province, as determined by international and national sample testing, was the only jurisdiction without any form of province-wide testing. In an attempt to assist its improvement efforts, this province was offered free access to standardized tests so that it could cross a threshold of internal resistance. This offer was eschewed specifically identifying negative political consequences from their teachers' union. *Benefits to students were deemed less important than benefits to politicians.*

Potential for cost savings is evident from research on standardized testing where costs in testing increased across the United States after the passage of the No Child Left Behind Act in 2002 (Vu, 2008). By 2008, state spending on testing increased from $423 million to almost $1.1 billion, or an increase of 160 percent, compared with an inflation increase of only 19.22 percent. Critics of standardized testing might want to condemn this eight-fold increase; however, the increase actually accentuates the validity for instituting *common assessment* across the country. *Replicating test construction in each state is financial foolishness.*

During the time when Canadian bureaucrats discussed common assessment, Canadian news media were already focusing public attention on provincial results from national and international assessments. Some provincial governments, already criticized for their poor results, were not amenable to providing additional opportunity when media could draw public attention to their education system's lack of success. Criticisms regarding poor results could be explained away by indicating that these tests were only from a *sample of students*, and the tests' margin of error was quite significant.

Launching a testing program that involved *all* students was a considerable concern because the effect of *educational leadership* could be assessed more readily. Every parent would have a personal interest in news stories related to interprovincial comparisons because they could compare their child's results across the nation. Evidence that their province's schools employed lower standards relative to other regions across the country could be more apparent because teachers were *more generous in their marking* revealing the degree of grade inflation.

The sample testing through national and international testing was already revealing inflated marking to be a problem. For example, Alberta's students repeatedly scored the highest levels of achievement on these national tests but surveys regarding students' marks revealed that Alberta's students received the lowest marks from their classroom teachers. Provincial testing served as a *check and balance* for the rampant grade inflation tendencies across the country. *Grade inflation in the school system is a serious problem which everyone in the education system wants kept out of the public forum.*

The committee of provincial curriculum representatives referenced earlier met three times per year over the course of several years but came to an abrupt halt shortly after this discussion regarding the potential for a common curriculum leading to common assessment. *Providing the public with the capacity to measure the quality of leadership was too threatening.* Governments like to espouse a commitment to their students' best interests but, in reality, they were more committed to their own interests for reelection. *Providing comparability of results has the potential to reveal whether the government's priority is their clients—taxpayer, parents, and students—or their own self-interest for reelection.*

A decade later, a parallel issue emerged in the United States—another of the few countries where the constitution identifies *state powers over federal jurisdiction in education.* As already demonstrated, poor national results on international tests prompted the national governors' council to pursue a coordinated effort toward improving student achievement. A consortium of forty-five governors signed on to develop common standards in reading and math, and then pilot common assessments for measuring student gains in achievement that would be incorporated into teacher evaluations.

State governors requested *common standards*—formally known as Common Core—and the Department of Education, under Secretary Arne Duncan, pursued the concepts *of common assessment* and *teachers' evaluations including results about student achievement*—that is, test scores. No Child Left Behind, a *bi-partisan initiative* lead by a Republican president, George W. Bush, and supported by a Democrat senator, Ted Kennedy, increased the level of federal involvement in America's education system. Dueck (2016) documents the considerable backlash from politicians and their constituents regarding this increased federal government involvement.

In November, 2015, after spending many years in partisan wrangling over a rewrite of education policy, Congress negotiators reached an agreement summarized by Troyan (2015) in USA Today:

- States will set and enforce their own K–12 academic standards.
- The new law maintains the federal regimen of 17 reading, math, and science tests in Grades 3 through 12 but leaves it to the states to decide how to use those scores to hold schools accountable.
- No Child Left Behind was praised for raising expectations and setting high standards, but it fell out of favor with educators and parents for its intense focus on testing and heavy-handed accountability rules.

- Democrats and Republicans generally agreed the replacement bill should shift some power away from Washington and back to local school districts. The US education secretary can no longer push for academic standards like the Common Core or mandate that teachers be evaluated based on things like student test scores.
- Under the new K–12 law, school districts identified by their states as underperforming will be eligible for federal grants to make improvements, but the federal government will not prescribe which reforms are necessary.
- The deal also will bar the US Education Department from requiring states to adopt Common Core academic standards in exchange for federal grants. They want the federal government out of the business of identifying failing schools, leaving that tough job to the states. Each state will come up with its own plan to help schools improve, its own deadlines, and its own metrics to measure that improvement. If schools don't improve, states will have to figure out what to do.
- John Kline, R-Minn., chairman of the House education committee said Congress has a chance "to replace a failed approach to education with a new approach that will reduce the federal role, restore local control, and empower parents."

The possibility of *comparability is frightening to the education system*, whether it is in Canada or in the United States. The American bill passed and still allows governors to undertake consortia activities, which they accomplished originally with Common Core—a concept abandoned earlier in Canada. Additionally, the matter of leaving regions responsible for holding schools accountable can be accommodated by states becoming a consortium, albeit *this is highly unlikely without some external pressure* applied from another body such as a federal government.

In reality, *the American Congress and president wilted from placing students at the top of the education pyramid*. One end of the political spectrum is concerned with the federal office exercising too much leadership in the nation because it is attempting to raise educational standards across the country. *Ensuring educational fairness* for every American student regardless of their region is a low priority for too many politicians.

The other end of the political spectrum yielded to pressure from teachers' unions who persistently oppose using student outcomes in teacher evaluations and then actually incorporate these evaluations into teachers' pay. *Too many politicians pander for votes by disregarding the quality of teaching service provided to students and, in this vein of thinking, treat students unfairly by relegating them to the bottom of the education pyramid.*

Education serves a basic need in preparing the next generation of leaders, workers, and citizens; yet, there is satisfaction with operating a school system characterized by disparate levels of student success. National standards are deemed necessary for membership into the health and accounting professions. The automobile industry is required to meet standards as are the people intending to become drivers. Common standards are evident in the justice system, food industry, airline travel, building construction, etc. *However, educating the country's future citizens and leaders remains immune.*

The world is vastly different from the time when the constitutions of the United States and Canada were crafted. Communities generally were isolated fiefdoms and residents seldom strayed from their home base, which is no longer the norm. The Manage Your Career website on career statistics reports that more than half of American college graduates do not return to their home base, and that *the average worker currently holds ten different jobs before age forty, and this number is projected to grow with today's youngest workers holding twelve to fifteen jobs in their lifetime. Their research also reported that college graduates earn 75 percent more during their life time.*

Providing a school system with vastly disparate educational standards across the country is no longer an acceptable norm when young people are faced with so many occasions involving competitions for jobs. Yes, individual states and provinces can form consortia, as they did with the Common Core in the United States and the Pan-Canadian Assessment Program in Canada, but these are usually precipitated in an environment where some crisis is exposed.

STANDARDS CREEP CAN BE CURTAILED

Both countries are facing standards creep because this complex issue of grade inflation is not easily portrayed in a one-minute newscast. This malaise plays well into the agenda of the political spectrum, which openly curries the favor of teachers and their unions. Research demonstrates that common assessment reduces grade inflation (Bishop, 2005; Laurie, 2007; Lawson, 2013; Phelps, 2003; Dueck, 2014). In both countries, information regarding grade inflation is stifled from getting to the public because political parties are aligned with teachers' unions that represent a powerful political lobby and substantial voting bloc.

Common assessment is the necessary component for educational comparability, which involves the ongoing use of standardized assessments. Therefore, educators vilify tests that are given across student populations in an attempt to "kill the messenger," which are student achievement results from standardized tests (Phelps, 2003). *Without consistent assessment, comparability is negated and accountability is defeated.*

Greater misfortune for students occurs because they are denied the advantage available to them from participating in standardized testing programs.

According to a peer-reviewed, 100-year analysis of testing research completed in 2011 by testing scholar Richard P. Phelps, 93 percent of studies found student testing, including the use of large-scale and high-stakes standardized tests, to have a "positive effect" on student achievement. *Accountability is an investment and not an expense!* Fairness to students should be the political objective rather than appeasing special interests groups who shrink-away from accountability.

It is time that truth is spoken by having these types of meta analyses reach the public domain. *Truth does not take sides* (Leaks, 2010). However, people do, and education's leadership must be more active in ensuring that our political leadership is better informed even though such efforts may be unpopular with special interest organizations such as teachers' unions.

Courage to speak in support of standardized testing can be bolstered by other significant issues summarized in the ProCon.org website on standardized testing:

- Standardized tests are reliable and objective measures of student achievement. *Without them*, policy-makers would have to rely on tests scored by individual schools and teachers who have a vested interest in producing favorable results. Multiple-choice tests, in particular, are graded by machine and therefore are not subject to human subjectivity or bias (Phelps, 2002).
- Twenty school systems that "have achieved significant, sustained, and widespread gains" on national and international assessments used "proficiency targets for each school" and "frequent, standardized testing to monitor system progress," according to a 2010 report by McKinsey & Company, a global management consulting firm (Mourshed et al. 2010).
- *Most students believe standardized tests are fair.* A June 2006 Public Agenda survey of 1,342 public school students in Grades 6 through12 found that 71 percent of students think the number of tests they have to take is "about right" and 79 percent believe test questions are fair (Education Insights, 2006).
- Teacher-graded assessments are inadequate alternatives to standardized tests because they are subjectively scored and unreliable. Most teachers are not trained in testing and measurement, and *research has shown many teachers "consider non-cognitive outcomes, including student class participation, perceived effort, progress over the period of the course, and comportment," which are irrelevant to subject-matter mastery* (Phelps, 2011).
- Stricter standards and increased testing are better preparing school students for college. In January 1998, Public Agenda found that 66 percent of college professors said "elementary and high schools expect students to learn too little." By March 2002, after a surge in testing and the passing of NCLB, that figure dropped to 47 percent "in direct support of higher

expectations, strengthened standards and better tests" (Public Agenda, 2002) (Gerstner, 2002).
- *Many objections voiced by the antitesting movement are really objections to NCLB's use of test results, not to standardized tests themselves.* Prominent testing critic Diane Ravitch, research professor of education at New York University, concedes standardized testing has value: "Testing . . . is not the problem . . . information derived from tests can be extremely valuable, if the tests are valid and reliable." She cites the NAEP as a positive example, and says tests can "inform educational leaders and policy-makers about the progress of the education system as a whole" (Ravitch, 2010).
- The multiple-choice format used on standardized tests produces accurate information necessary to assess and improve American schools. According to the Center for Teaching Excellence at the University of Illinois at Urbana-Champaign, multiple-choice questions can provide "highly reliable test scores" and an "objective measurement of student achievement" (Center for Teaching Excellence, 2011). Today's multiple-choice tests are more sophisticated than their predecessors. The Center for Public Education, a national public school advocacy group, says many "multiple-choice tests now require considerable thought, even notes and calculations, before choosing a bubble" (Mitchell, 2006).
- *Most parents approve of standardized tests.* A June–July 2013 Associated Press-NORC Center for Public Affairs Research poll found that 75 percent of parents say standardized tests "are a solid measure of their children's abilities" and 69 percent say the tests "are a good measure of the schools' quality." Ninety-three percent of parents say standardized tests "should be used to identify areas where students need extra help" and 61 percent say their children "take an appropriate number of standardized tests" (Elliott and Agiesta, 2013).
- Increased testing does not force teachers to encourage "drill 'n' kill" rote learning. According to a study in the October 28, 2005, issue of the peer-reviewed *Education Policy Analysis Archives*, good teachers understand that "isolated drills on the types of items expected on the test" are unacceptable, and principals interviewed said "they would sanction any teacher caught teaching to the test" (Yeh, 2005). In any case, research has shown that drilling students does not produce test score gains: "teaching a curriculum aligned to state standards and using test data as feedback produces higher test scores than an instructional emphasis on memorization and test-taking skills" (Barth and Mitchell, 2006).
- Standardized tests provide a lot of useful information at low cost, and consume little class time (Walberg, 2011). According to a 2002 paper by Hoxby, and Bommer, professor in economics at Stanford University, standardized tests cost less than 0.1 percent of K–12 education spending, totaling $5.81

per student per year: "Even if payments were 10 times as large, they would still not be equal to 1 percent of what American jurisdictions spend on education" (Hoxby, 2002). Other cost estimates range from $15–$33 per student per year by the nonpartisan US Government Accountability Office (GAO), to as low as $2 per student per year by testing scholar and economist Richard Phelps (Phelps, 2002). A 50-item standardized test can be given in an hour and is graded instantaneously by computer (Walberg, 2011).
- China has a long tradition of standardized testing and leads the world in educational achievement. China displaced Finland as number one in reading, math, and science when Shanghai debuted on the PISA rankings in 2009 (Dillon, 2010). Despite calls for a reduction in standardized testing, China's testing regimen remains firmly in place (Xueqin, 2010). Chester E. Finn Jr., chairman of the Hoover Institution's Koret Task Force on K–12 Education, predicts that Chinese cities will top the PISA charts for the next several decades (Dillon, 2010).
- *"Teaching to the test" can be a good thing because it focuses on essential content and skills, eliminates time-wasting activities that don't produce learning gains, and motivates students to excel* (Barth and Mitchell, 2006). The US Department of Education stated in November 2004, "If teachers cover subject matter required by the standards and teach it well, then students will master the material on which they will be tested—and probably much more" (US Department of Education, 2004).
- *Standardized tests are not narrowing the curriculum, rather they are focusing it on important basic skills all students need to master.* According to a study in the October 28, 2005, issue of the peer-reviewed *Education Policy Analysis Archives*, teachers in four Minnesota school districts said standardized testing had a positive impact, improving the quality of the curriculum while raising student achievement (Yeh, 2005).
- Most teachers acknowledge the importance of standardized tests and do not feel that their teaching has been compromised. In a 2009 Scholastic/Gates Foundation survey, 81 percent of US public school teachers said state-required standardized tests were at least "somewhat important" as a measure of students' academic achievement, and 27 percent said they were "very important" or "absolutely essential" (Scholastic and the Bill and Melinda Gates Foundation, 2010). Seventy-three percent of teachers surveyed in a March, 2002, Public Agenda study said they "have not neglected regular teaching duties for test preparation" (Public Agenda 2002).
- An oft-cited Arizona State University study in *EPAA*'s March 28, 2002, edition, concluding that testing has little educational merit, has been discredited by educational researchers for poor methodology, and was criticized for wrongly blaming the tests themselves for stagnant test scores, rather than the shortcomings of teachers and schools (Haney, 2006).

These are some of the studies that need to be explained in the public arena. Interest groups afraid of comparability, because of the pressure these create to improve performance for the fairness and benefit of students, are doing their utmost to challenge the use of standardized tests. As important as these studies are, *there is one major fact that refutes the claims of groups seeking to discredit standardized tests.* Incredulously, the loud voices of minority positions outweigh those of the silent majority.

ALLIANCE OF ANXIETY

Overwhelmingly, teachers believe in standardized testing. They use them all of the time with their students. In simplest terms, a standardized test is any assessment given to two or more students. *Whenever teachers give a spelling test, basic facts test, end-of-chapter test, work sheets, unit tests, end-of-year tests, etc., to a group of students in a class or in multiple classes, they are utilizing a standardized test.* In other words, teachers could be using dozens of standardized tests every year.

Standardized testing is not the controversial issue that educators and their unions want to portray. *They are merely attempting to confuse the public about the real issue, which is the use of a standardized test for two or more classrooms where different teachers are involved.* Whenever standardized assessments involve two or more classrooms in a school, district, state or province, or across the country, comparability is possible. In the mind of too many educators, *the villain is comparability*, and permitting its use raises stress levels.

The potential for comparability in measuring student success creates anxiety for educators—teachers, principals, district administrators, state or provincial administrators—as well as for politicians at these levels, because there is potential to *quantify their leadership. This feature, where the performance of practitioners, administrators, and politicians are all impacted by test results, places these three groups in an alliance of anxiety. This alliance effectively keeps the media from fulfilling their responsibility in promoting transparency in educational issues.*

An example of this anxiety was expressed earlier in this chapter when discussing the work of provincial education bureaucrats in Canada. Their opposition to a national curriculum evident in almost all countries of the world, was based on *their fear* of common assessment. *Comparability of results was their villain.* When teachers are not getting the job done, administrators' actions come under scrutiny and, when a school system is underperforming, politicians feel the pressure of accountability. *They are obligated to act if they value their children.*

This *alliance of anxiety* faced by those involved within the education system can intimidate anyone from breaking away and pursuing greater accountability. Canada is the only country in the world without a federal presence in education. Therefore, each province over samples during international assessments in order to qualify as a separate country and receive results. In 2003, Alberta's PISA results were the highest in the world; slightly higher than Finland which had the highest national results.

Alberta's success was precipitated by implementing province-wide standardized testing a few years earlier in language arts, mathematics, science, and social studies, which quickly produced dramatic gains in student achievement. Other provinces consulted with Alberta and followed suit with their own assessment program, and dozens of countries sent representatives to understand the *Alberta advantage*.

One delegation from the United Kingdom included the minister of education who requested a meeting with several sections within Alberta's Department of Education. The assembly met but the administrator responsible for accountability and transparency was not available to participate until an hour into the meeting. When entering the room, the minister interrupted the conversation and pronounced, "You, sir, are the reason for my being here personally."

This minister then made a profound explanation: "Ostensibly we—The UK team—are here to talk about English as a Second Language and technology programs, but the real purpose is to talk about accountability in education." His explanation included the *ruse* used in announcing his excursion to Alberta so that teachers' unions and media in the United Kingdom would think that the trip was for purposes other than accountability. The intimidation from teachers' unions made it necessary to keep secret that portion of the agenda that would create backlash back home.

This story did not end there, however. The minister, having heard the story about how excellent results were achieved, extended an invitation to meet in the House of Commons in London. The specific purpose was to "infect senior education bureaucrats" with the story so that they, too, would embark on a journey despite opposition forces in that country. A few months later a lengthy discussion with the minister and his staff took place in the House of Commons.

An additional event occurred shortly thereafter. The office of the UK prime minister requested additional discussion so that the highest office in the country could also become familiar with Alberta's success. This follow-up occurred shortly thereafter with several of his representatives journeying to Alberta.

The point in this story is that the *education system experiences considerable intimidation for anyone attempting to incorporate greater levels of accountability and transparency.* Standardized testing, while used extensively throughout the school system, produces immense anxiety when these tests are given across many classes, schools, districts, states or provinces, and countries. *Comparability of results is the issue rather than standardized testing.*

Implementing common standards, as well as increasing students' success in achieving these, is a significant factor available in moving beyond a balanced scorecard to an environment where the results are also assessed. *Comparability across the state and province is enhanced by leaders nationalizing a report card and increasing pressure on the education system across the nations to achieve.* Comparability provides taxpayers and parents with data to pose the question: *"If there, why not here?"*

There is a glimmer of hope emerging in the United States. Chapter 1 indicates how states systematically reduced levels of difficulty in their examinations to qualify for No Child Left Behind grants. The Common Core combined with common assessment were introduced to combat this *fraudulent behavior. Education Next* published the grades given to state proficiency standards on an A-to-F scale designed by researchers in the Program on Education Policy and Governance (PEPG) at Harvard University:

Each state earns a grade according to the size of the difference between the percentages of students identified as proficient by state and by NAEP exams in

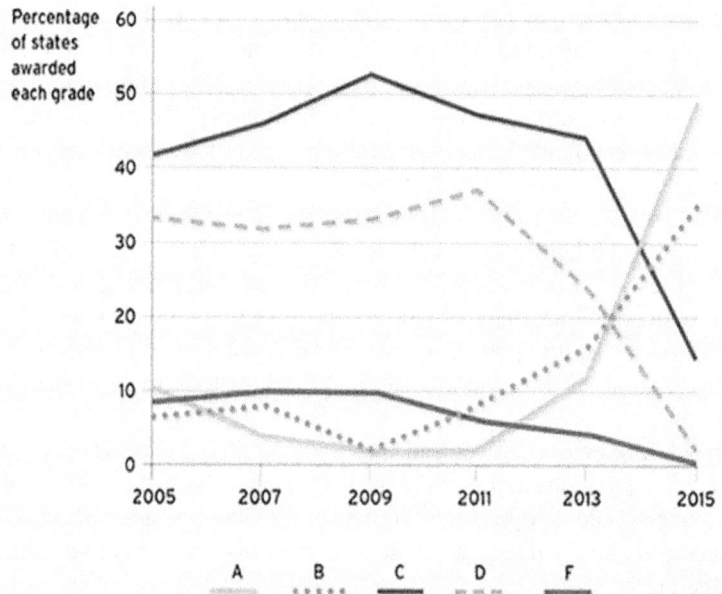

Figure 4.1   Percentages of States Awarded Grades Comparing State with NAEP Exams

4th- and 8th-grade math and reading. . . . In 2015, 24 of the 49 states (including the District of Columbia) for which data were available as of mid-January 2016 earned an "A." Meanwhile, the number of states receiving a "D" or an "F" has dwindled from 17 and 13 in 2005 and 2011, respectively, to a grand total of 1 in 2015 (See Figure 4.1). In short, state standards have suddenly skyrocketed. . . . *The Common Core consortium has achieved one of its key policy objectives: the raising of state proficiency standards throughout much of the United States.* (Peterson et al., 2016)

Learning well, living well is a meaningful objective for our global village environment but it requires decisive actions from political leaders *who are committed to replacing special interest groups at the top of the political pyramid with students*. This shift will only be accomplished when leadership becomes fully accountable and transparent, and school performance data is *not* kept a state secret. Federal office leadership to implement greater levels of comparability is not a requirement but courageous leadership across regions is.

KEY POINTS

- Comparability is the way of life in the private sector but resisted in the education system.
- Providing a comprehensive report on performance is essential and building comparability across the largest geographical region possible strengthens accountability and transparency.
- The public, especially parents, want information reported in a consistent manner to prevent confusion and misunderstanding.
- North American Constitutions delegate responsibility for education to states and provinces, which hinders progress toward establishing accountability through comparability.
- Canadian provinces rejected common curriculum because this made common assessment possible and results could be compared.
- The United States had some federal involvement through No Child Left Behind but, when governors requested Common Core (standards), the reaction toward a more national approach was shunted.
- Common assessment ensures comparability of standards and achieves accountability.
- Teachers routinely use standardized testing while criticizing their use when given to a large number of classes, which provides the opportunity to compare results.

Chapter 5

Choice

A Democratic Right

Ensuring that *all students* receive a *minimum standard* of education is a primary responsibility of government. Generally speaking, schools are their vehicle for accommodating this mandate and significant amounts of tax dollars go toward constructing and staffing these facilities. Therefore, *ownership of these schools* is an important issue and parents have a right to question authorities representing the government when children are *restricted to a specific facility*. The politically correct expectation is that parents merely accept placement decisions regardless of whether their child's educational needs are adequately addressed.

While many contentious issues dominate the education environment, few are more sensitive than the issue of school choice. Our school system's history is dominated by a culture where most students were *required* to attend the neighborhood school, unless they were designated as special needs children and bussed to a magnet center for similarly designated students across a larger region. The only other opportunity for parents wishing to exercise choice was to opt out of the publicly funded school system and enroll children in private schools.

Choice opens the door to competition and allows parents to shop around for services and programs they believe will be in their child's best interests. Providing parents with the opportunity to shop around opens the door to free market principles we explore in our daily living. We would object to being restricted to a state-designated grocery store. Limiting choice in clothing, a distinctive feature in pursuing individuality, would produce rebellion in all age groups and sectors of our society. *Choice is cherished* and not something our political leaders dare hinder.

In education, however, there has been a discernible disinterest by many governments to employ free market principles. There are several smoke screens that obscure their political objective and that they can hide behind, while preventing education's clients—that is, parents—from exercising a fundamental democratic principle. Issues regarding space in existing school facilities, transportation costs, and balance in ethnic or racial diversity are examples used to *deflect parents from pursuing what they believe will be in their child's best interests.*

The annual PDK/Gallup poll for 2015 sums up the public's mood for choice and the challenge that governments face. Nearly two-thirds of Americans favor permitting parents to select any public school in their district, support that's relatively consistent across racial groups (Q15). Six in ten public school parents said they have enough information about the public schools to make an informed choice about their child's school (Q16).

Of eleven factors presented, public school parents believe the *three most important factors* in choosing a local public school include the quality of the teachers, the curriculum (i.e., the courses offered), and the *maintenance of student discipline* (Q17). The curriculum is an important issue for high school and a student's interest in career; however, the other two factors are critical at all grade levels, and are directly related to the quality of education available at the school.

Parents want the right to escape from learning environments where their child is going to be disadvantaged, and governments are challenged in their politically correct posture of keeping too many students prisoner. Public education should be obligated to provide parents with cost-free alternatives rather than pushing concerned parents toward the private school system. Governments seriously pursuing transformational change in education should provide parents with a right to choose their child's school.

UNIONS' FEARS VERSUS PARENTS' CHOICES

Teachers' unions and their opposition to educational reform is the political motivation behind the many blockages parents face while pursuing school choice. Unions are unified in their resistance exemplified by opposing any amounts of public funding to independent schools, even though the *public purse saves money when parents exercise choice* and contribute significant personal funds. The public is easily fooled when unions chant, "No public dollars for private schooling." Their connotation is that a segment of the population is benefitting financially from attending private education.

Parents, pursuing an option for private schooling, understand how they are double-taxed because they pay taxes for public education as well as fees for their child's enrolment in private education. *They are challenging a notion that all schools are equally effective,* and they are willing to pay extra dollars for acquiring educational services beyond what they believe is available in their local school.

District administrators are well aware that schools are not equally effective but their perceptions usually remain confidential. Revelations concerning the substantial variances in quality of educational services could be a career-limiting move in a politically correct environment where administrators' evaluations usually are influenced by staff's perceptions.

Charter schools, another venture for disrupting educational monopolies, were instituted in the United States during reform efforts in the 1990s, and public support for this option has been growing steadily since their inception in 1992. By 2000, approximately 2,000 charter schools were in place increasing to 6,004 by 2012–2013, serving more than 2.2 million students in 42 states and Washington, DC. Parents are voting with their feet.

Public support is not linked with union support, however. Teachers Union Website on January 13, 2016, contained a page, "Teachers Unions Oppose Education Reform" wherein they described the control union leaders exercised on politicians.

> The control that union officials can maintain over local school boards borders on the ridiculous. Veteran education reporter Joe Williams wrote: "The United Teachers Los Angeles had such a tight grip on its school board in 2004 that union leaders actually instructed them on important policies and made no attempt to hide their hand signals to school board members during meetings.
>
> Regardless of one's view of any particular method of improving America's struggling public schools (whether school choice, charter schools, or rewarding better teachers with better pay), the tactics and rhetoric that teachers' unions employ to block any meaningful reform is remarkable. Their motivation is simple: maintain the status quo—*and the flow of hundreds of millions of dollars in dues*. Meanwhile, union leaders' suggestions for reform are best summarized as "more money to hire more teachers," who are then likely to become dues-paying union members.

Fitzgerald (2013) reported that money is the bottom line with labor leaders who worry about the public's flight to choice: "Labor leaders say they want to organize charter schools because teachers are complaining about low pay and poor working conditions. Some observers, though, say the push toward unionization is to help unions boost their declining membership rolls." With only about 12 percent of charter school staff unionized, both teachers' unions have lost approximately 3 percent from 2011, according to the Department of Labor.

Critics within the education system attempt to portray that charter schools "cream" more advantaged students from the traditional public schools. A report by Rebarber and Zgainer (2014) puts to *rest the myth that charter students are cherry-picked and less disadvantaged than students in traditional public schools:*

> Charter students are somewhat more likely to qualify for Free and Reduced Lunch due to being low-income (63 percent of charter students versus 48 percent of public school students), to being African-American (28 percent of charter students versus 16 percent of public school students) or to being Hispanic (28 percent of charter students versus 23 percent of public school students).
>
> Many charter schools, especially those in urban environments, serve concentrated low-income and at-risk student populations. Sixty-one percent of charter schools serve student populations where more than 60 percent of students qualify for the Free and Reduced lunch program for low-income families. Similarly, 27 percent of charter schools serve populations with at least 60 percent of students categorized as at-risk.

These authors also provide data that explains how teachers' working conditions in charter schools support higher standards of accountability. The overwhelming majority of charter schools have been nonunion since the early days of the charter movement and the small percentage that were unionized are declining to record lows of approximately 11 percent.

The percentage of charter schools implementing skill-based and performance-based staff contracts has increased to 39 percent for the former and to 37 percent for the latter. Rebarber and Zgainer indicate that these increases are a positive trend that shows how, when given freedom, charter schools take hold of their own staffing authority and create a salary system based on skills and performance, and reject the fixed salary levels that have been comfortably adhered to and influenced by teachers' unions to ensure uniformity across all public schools.

Many students are overwhelmed by the *pace of learning* required and can benefit from additional *time for learning*. We have already indicated how today's curriculum is expanded to assume societal needs beyond basic education. Considerably more learning and development is packed into today's schooling but without additional time provided. In 2014, 27 percent of charter schools provided an extended school year and 48 percent increased the length of their school day.

Charter schools are accountable for student achievement. Their rules and structure are dependent on state-authorizing legislation, which differs across states. A charter school is authorized to function once it has received a charter, a statutorily defined performance contract detailing the school's mission, program, goals, students served, methods of assessment, and *ways to measure success*. The length of time for which charters are granted varies, but most are granted for three to five years, which requires a degree of success to not face closure.

Accountability requires consequences when mandates are not achieved. As of March 2009, 12.5 percent of the over 5000 charter schools founded in the United States had closed for reasons including academic, financial, and managerial problems, and occasionally consolidation or district interference (Allen, 2009). This same level of accountability would produce dramatic educational reforms across America's public school system.

The critical conclusion in discussing charter schools is that they are flourishing across the United States as parents make choices in schooling for their children. *Parents from all backgrounds are opting out of their restrictive public schools in order to take advantage of educational programming free from union control and more committed to serving their clients.*

In Canada, only Alberta's government embraced charter schools and Bennett (2010) describes educators' responses to Alberta's initiative:

When the Alberta government of Ralph Klein authorized Canada's first charter schools, the core interests in Canadian education (school superintendents, education faculties, and teachers' unions) *closed ranks and successfully fended off charter schools everywhere else.* Instead of fairly evaluating charters as a means of broadening school choice, public school authorities *clicked into siege mentality mode*, condemning the "privatizers" and casting aspersions on the motives of charter school advocates.

Bennett further indicates that this option for parents remains "a well-kept secret" to the rest of the country.

Notwithstanding that charter schools experienced limited access into Canada, the movement in the United States prompted Edmonton Public Schools (EPS) in Alberta to take dramatic action for promoting school choice. In the late 1990s, EPS was heralded by researchers for implementing site-based decision making and *open boundaries for school choice.* Reformers focused on these processes from philosophical perspectives *without access to data* on the implications for student achievement because universal provincial testing was in its infancy.

EPS, with approximately 80,000 students, is unique because parents had the second lowest level of socioeconomic status (SES) in the province. A very small district of 2000 students serving villages across Northern Alberta was the only one of 62 districts with a lower SES. EPS was essentially an inner-city school district encircled by several smaller cities with exceptionally high SES.

Subsequently, provincial testing in Grade 3 placed EPS results below the provincial mean but well up from the bottom: a result which *exceeded expectations.* By Grade 6, student achievement was consistently above the provincial mean, and by Grade 9 achievement levels were consistently higher. In Grade 12, diploma examination results for graduates leaving EPS were in the upper quartile for the province. *The longer period of time students attended EPS schools the higher were their levels of achievement.*

During these years, parents exercised their right to choose schools with approximately 50 percent of students enrolled in a school outside their neighborhood. During this time, 94 percent of students across Canada and 86 percent across Alberta attended their neighborhood school. Parents and their children in EPS were well served by the open-boundary approach, which instilled a level of competition within the school district.

Providing choice is a significant factor in improving educational outcomes. When parents can exercise choice in schools, their involvement is greater, while students demonstrate higher levels of motivation because their talent can be more closely aligned with a school's mission. Where districts endeavor to provide some choice, constraints that prevent the majority of students from experiencing the benefits of choice are frequently evident.

Transportation is a major inhibitor against choice; however, this cost item can be overcome. A point was made earlier that school districts seldom cut programs and services when contemplating additional ones. New programs usually require additional staff, which reduces workloads across the school system, and even parents are pleased because they are led to believe that reduced workloads will benefit students. The point is that choice improves the education system and school districts are wise to increase this emphasis even if it requires transferring funds from other programs yielding little return on investment.

Providing choice in school registration means increased student mobility. Occasionally walk limits may accommodate more than one school *but choice should include the opportunity to engage in programs much farther away.* Students from disadvantaged homes likely cannot afford transportation fares and, therefore, are too frequently excluded from pursuing choices. When administration is *mandated to accommodate choice for all students at zero cost for transportation,* creativity can derive many options to accommodate this strategy which has a payback in significantly higher levels of engagement and motivation.

The critical points in this chapter are three-fold:

1. Lack of choice inhibits accountability and improvement. Choice facilitates competition within the education system and energizes creativity for reform. *Therefore, governments should expand choice by supporting private schools and charter schools.*
2. Choice within a school system can be increased by removing restrictive attendance boundaries where space permits. *Therefore, parents should be*

encouraged to place their child in a public school they believe is more aligned with their child's needs.
3. An open-boundary system is unfair to less-advantaged children who are unable to find or fund transportation. *Therefore, school districts should provide transportation for students to other schools where space permits.* This is a cost item that can be funded by savings outlined in chapter 17.

Philosophical barriers raised by politically correct thinking have failed parents' right to pursue the best education environment for their child. Providing parents with choice introduces competition into a system where instituting reform is difficult and, when parents have unfettered choice, there are higher levels of accountability for people and institutions providing educational services.

KEY POINTS

- Many contentious issues dominate the education environment but few are more sensitive than the issue of school choice.
- Teachers' unions oppose choice because it opens the door to competition and greater levels of accountability.
- Charter schools are flourishing in the United States and are meeting the educational needs of a diversified student population.
- All schools can increase choice by removing school boundaries when space permits.
- All students, especially those from disadvantaged homes, should benefit from increased choice by having transportation requirements accommodated without cost.

Chapter 6

Coaches Are Not Evaluators

We cannot trust even well-intentioned people if they are not good at what they are doing. Effective, highly interactive cultures incorporate pressure and high support; it is impossible not to notice whether someone is doing great work or bad work. Because people in these cultures know that improvement is tough going and that disagreement is a normal part of any change, they are more inclined and prepared to confront it. Students, parents and colleagues know when bad teaching is being tolerated. (Fullan, 2005)

Well-intentioned school principals are in an untenable position today and it seriously degrades their school's effectiveness. On the one hand, they are required to lead through influence and trust while on the other they are to assess and evaluate in ways that could end a colleague's career. Is it realistic to think that a person can cultivate friendship and support one day while confronting mediocrity on the next?

Coaching, a fundamental responsibility assigned to principals, requires a relationship of integrity developed over time, but can this bond be cultivated when both parties *know assessment devoid of personal feeling is also required*? This chapter argues that it is *unrealistic to expect principals to play both roles* and that by insisting on it, we have opted for an approach that ultimately *tolerates bad teaching*. The current model is another example of teachers rather than students being atop education's pyramidal pinnacle.

THE ROLE OF RELATIONSHIPS IN INFLATED ASSESSMENT

A propensity for teachers to inflate grades linked to their students' achievement is a significant issue (Dueck 2014; Phelps 2013). Teachers spend all of their time coaching students on ways to succeed and to reach their potential;

then, we ask them to assume the mantle of an evaluator who will assess the degree to which learning is achieved. Consequently, significant levels of *grade inflation* occur and the whole process of having teachers acting as the *sole evaluator* of their own students is called into question. This is one of the reasons the educational system has to incorporate *large-scale assessment and empirical evidence.*

Teaching is a relational activity and being the conveyor of bad news is difficult. Informing students that they are failing to attain grade-level standards and how repeating a course would be in their best interests is difficult. Social promotion alleviated the problem and enabled the school *to avoid being held accountable for student achievement* and for the emotional trauma of separating students out from a peer group: albeit with a group functioning at a similar stage in their learning.

Relationships interfere with objectivity. Society, in general, understands this reality and sets up criteria to take it into account. For example, obtaining a driver's license is a significant milestone on the path to adulthood. Parents are often involved in coaching their children to become good drivers. Accountability is high because the parent is obviously concerned about the safety of their child, but they are also concerned about the possibility of damage to their vehicle and the potential impact this will have on their insurance coverage. Motivation to provide good coaching is at a high level, and many parents wisely reach out to others, such as a driver training instructor, for assistance.

Our governments do not accept that a parent's high sense of accountability and motivation to ensure their son or daughter learns to drive well is reason to entrust them with the responsibility to determine if their child is ready for a driver's license. On the contrary, qualifying for a driver's license requires passing a standardized test as well as a practical road experience with an examiner, who makes the final determination about readiness. A passing certificate, or driver's license, is only granted when potentially biased interpersonal relationships are removed. Even driver trainers as coaches are considered too close to the student to give the final verdict.

In sports, the usual model in managing teams is to separate the coaching role from the selection process. Coaches manage the team in the sense of determining who will play what position and which players will be on the field of play at a given point in time. Between games they instruct players on how they can perform more effectively, and use a variety of strategies to maximize the player's motivation.

However, someone with a higher level of responsibility and a greater sense of objectivity decides who can wear the team uniform. General managers coordinate player selection and deselection processes including trades. These processes undoubtedly incorporate coaches' opinions, but the general manager is expected to provide the team's coach or manager with the best player talent given the resources available. The general manager is also responsible to the team's president or owner to manage the coaches so performance throughout the organization is maximized.

In some areas of the private sector the coach and evaluator are conflated, but this is normal because the bottom line (profit) acts as an independent *arbiter of performance*. There is a far more discernible bottom line where profit and loss is the significant measure. An owner is compelled to move quickly when employees are not doing the job efficiently and effectively. Underperformance in the private sector has the capacity to imperil the entire operation, so accountability is relatively simple and straightforward.

Teachers and school administrators, along with most other public employees, have been successful at resisting this model of accountability. *Educators focus more on process than on student outcomes, especially those related to academic achievement.* Too frequently they look to blame the home for ineffective parenting or the government for providing insufficient funding. Blame is assigned to the student for his or her lack of motivation rather than to the teachers' lack of effort and teaching talent.

Principals lack of bottom-line measurement data related to student outcomes are reduced to *measuring the processes teachers use in their classroom*. They measure these against their own standards on how well these processes are applied but their judgments are clouded by their own philosophy regarding which teacher practices are the most suitable for student success. Within all of this activity, as well intentioned as it may be, there is a greater personal problem that principals must overcome.

While fulfilling their *coaching role*, principals have to build trust with teachers by forging strong relationships. Like teachers, when assessing their students, principals believe they do an excellent job at coaching in preparation for the evaluation. Recognizing shortcomings in their clients' abilities can be interpreted as proving their coaching efforts were not effective. Not surprisingly they see some scant evidence of effective teaching and inflate the degree to which the teacher actually can apply it consistently.

THE "BACK SCRATCH EFFECT"

The entire teacher supervision process is tainted further by a wrongheaded focus on how the principal is evaluated by the very same people he or she is evaluating, namely teachers. In essence, this approach is characterized by *I'll scratch your back if you scratch mine*. This conflict of interest should, by itself, be sufficient to end the practice *unless the educational system incorporates a check-and-balance approach with a principal evaluation model that focuses primarily on student outcomes in the school.*

Such a model, where coaches evaluate their direct reports, is also an issue in school district offices. One superintendent commented that she instituted a five-level scale evaluation model for her assistant superintendents. It was the first time empirical data sources gleaned from client satisfaction surveys were used in the district. These evaluations were not just a pass/fail model, but utilized the five-level scale ranging from "excellent" to "less than satisfactory."

Based on the data as well as her observations, she identified several areas with each subordinate where work performance was solid but not demonstrating excellence. On this basis, the overall performance was rated as "very good." These assistant superintendents were not pleased that their evaluations left them with ratings below "excellent." It was standard practice in surrounding districts to evaluate senior staff as "excellent," and these specific senior staff worried that a rating less than the norm could negatively impact their career opportunities.

In essence, senior staff believed an "excellent" performance rating was their *entitlement. The politically correct action was to provide the norm.* Introducing empirical data made it impossible for evaluators to come to a conclusion where everyone was assessed "excellent" because the data differentiated employees on the basis of performance. This superintendent blazed a trail of nonconformity and she would pay the price. Those who were disgruntled with her objective evaluation formed a small, disloyal alliance and waited until it was their turn to evaluate her and settle the score.

At the school level, *the problem is that principals provide high ratings for their teachers because teachers will rate them when their leadership is evaluated by district leaders*. This pattern of behavior is replicated further up the hierarchy as assistant superintendents want high evaluations from their principals when the superintendent is conducting their performance reviews. Similarly, the superintendent is anticipating loyalty from underlings when the school board is reviewing his or her leadership. Everyone is looking to have "their back scratched." Once again, standards suffer because performance levels are inflated.

The proof of how ineffective the current evaluation process for educators is can be found in the deselection data. The current model is not weeding out ineffective teachers because standards are too low. Principals are not "calling a spade a spade." The educational system places too much emphasis on staff relationships to the detriment of student outcomes. In the area of teacher supervision, *the educational system is once again arranged in a way that not only falls short of the student's best interest, but also runs counter to it.*

This unfortunate reality, *where relationships blind objectivity,* supports the union's primary objective, which is to look after the welfare of their members. They are not committed to looking after the best interests of the system's clients by ridding classrooms of ineffective practitioners. Neither are they supportive of using large-scale testing programs to identify weak teachers who may need to feel some pressure to improve. *Unions cannot pursue simultaneously the best interests of their members and the system's clients.* Their conflict of interest is self-evident.

This is depressingly easy to illustrate. One superintendent spoke of his experience with the union at the negotiating table. The union's position was that all teachers are "excellent," but that *management is to blame for the poor level of service from some because teachers were not placed properly where they can excel.* The teacher might function more effectively if there were fewer students in the class or with fewer students demonstrating special needs. The union's perspective was that the superintendent was not making sufficient effort to place the teacher in situations where his or her capacity for excellence could be displayed.

Why are state politicians so complacent about this clearly inadequate system of staff supervision? One of the most obvious reasons is that their governance structure also operates without adequate concern for the bottom line. Public sector enterprises share a common ethos, and politicians looking to "right the ship" in education would have to "right their own" first. In other words, they would have to tackle the self-centeredness of their own government's unions first, and then deal directly with the ensuing conflict.

Well-intentioned incompetence is a major issue imperiling our society. Courage is a virtue we want all politicians to demonstrate, but it is rare, particularly when their political careers are always at stake. This explains their propensity to spend on projects those who elected them favor, and it explains why they are reticent to deal with complex and nebulous issues like staff supervision in schools, even though they might personally consider this an issue worthy of their attention.

School district officials associated with educational leadership are fairly knowledgeable about Superintendent Michelle Rhee's efforts to "weed-out" poor teachers in Washington, DC. She was known for her ability to remove poor teachers! In the end, the political heat her employers experienced was beyond their ability to endure. Having to choose between policies that championed students and those that favored interest groups, the school board waivered and then capitulated. Ms. Rhee went on to other educational endeavors.

Rhee was successful at least at one level: she used empirical evidence to show how bad the situation was and who the weak teachers were. *The critical point in this chapter is that coaches cannot evaluate unless they use empirical data to influence the evaluation process.* Data provides the basis for differentiated evaluations and the *likelihood of tension in working relationships.*

For principals to serve as effective team evaluators, they have to resort to empirical evidence, which is best for students in any case. Any other method of evaluation will lead to dysfunction. Even a simple statement that appears to have a negative connotation may produce conflict or even sever a relationship Once the relationship is damaged the principal will surely experience difficulty when it comes time for his or her assessment from the district office. The solution is to introduce higher levels of objectivity into the process.

REVEALING HIDDEN SECRETS OF A POOR EVALUATION SYSTEM

The media is now beginning to educate the public and provide for much greater transparency in the school system so that an informed public can influence developments in the school. *Waiting for "Superman,"* a pro-education reform documentary, indicated that one out of every 57 doctors loses his or her license to practice medicine; one out of every 97 lawyers loses his or her license to practice law; and in many major cities, only one out of 1000 teachers is fired for performance-related reasons.

Newspapers are now investigating the issue, and their findings are summarized on the Center for Union Facts website under the banner "Teachers Union Exposed":

- *The New York Daily News* reports that "over the past three years [2007–2010], just 88 out of some 80,000 (New York) city schoolteachers have lost their jobs for poor performance." (approximately 0.1 percent).
- The Albany *Times Union* looked at what was going on outside New York City and discovered that of 132,000 teachers; only 32 were fired for any reason between 2006 and 2011 (approximately 0.02 percent).
- In Chicago, *Newsweek* reported that only 0.1 percent of teachers were dismissed for performance-related reasons between 2005 and 2008. In a school district that has by any measure failed its students—only 28.5 percent of 11th graders met or exceeded expectations on that state's standardized tests. (The problem is worse than it seems because there are two Chicagos: north and south. In the north neighborhoods like Lincoln Park are found some of the highest performing schools. So how bad are the schools in the south? The averages make Chicago look bad, but the bad is far worse than the average.)
- *The Los Angeles Times* in 2009 reported that, in a school district where the graduation rate in 2003 was just 51 percent, between 1995 and 2005, only 112 tenured teachers in Los Angeles faced termination—eleven per year— out of 43,000 (approximately 0.03 percent annually).
- In ten years, only about 47 out of 100,000 teachers were actually terminated from New Jersey's schools (approximately 0.05 percent over 10 years).

- In any given year in Florida, scholar Richard Kahlenberg wrote, the involuntary dismissal rate for teachers was an abysmally low 0.05 percent, "compared with 7.9 percent in the Florida workforce as a whole."
- In Dallas, even when unofficial pressures to resign are factored in, only 0.78 percent of tenured teachers are terminated.
- Out of Tucson, Arizona's 2,300 tenured teachers, only seven have been fired for classroom behavior in the past five years (approximately 0.3 percent over 5 years).
- Des Moines, Iowa, a school district with almost 3,000 teachers, has fired just two for poor performance in five years (approximately 0.07 percent over 5 years).

Anderson (2013), a writer for the *New York Times*, reported that roughly 100 percent of teachers in Florida were deemed "effective" or "highly effective" in the most recent evaluations. Incredibly, teacher evaluations in 2011 typically involved a *single observation of about twenty minutes.* In Tennessee, 98 percent of teachers were judged to be "at expectations." In Michigan, 98 percent of teachers were rated "effective" or better. An official with the National Council on Teacher Quality conceded in an interview that "there are some alarm bells going off. . . . There's a real culture shift that has to occur and there's a lot of evidence that hasn't occurred yet."

What is the cultural shift that must happen? Even though some teacher evaluations are partly contingent on student test scores, they are mostly focused on principals' assessments acquired through their own observations of teachers. There is a need to abandon a culture where almost all teachers are considered *above average.*

Anderson points out how this problem of low standards is exacerbated by the involvement of evaluators "who generally are not detached managerial types and can be loath to give teachers low marks." Education is strengthened by having relational people working with students: it is weakened by requiring these well-intentioned people to "bell the cat" of mediocre colleagues. This emphasis on relationships is why there is not a substantial increase in the percentage of teachers who are removed from the classroom. This may also be why Florida's principals write their teachers' evaluations based on one twenty-minute observation.

When Anderson informed Grover J. Whitehurst, director of the Brown Center on Education Policy at the Brookings Institution that very few teachers were deemed "ineffective," he responded, "It would be an unusual profession that at least 5 percent are not deemed ineffective." Evaluating and developing talent is the most important management function in the educational system, whether it is occurring in the classroom with students by their teachers or with teachers by their principals. However, *low standards are endemic in the educational system* even though we claim that education is vital for our nation's future well-being.

Mellon (2010) explores the problem of low standards and asks why, in the past, teachers were rarely let go because of poor classroom performance. In an interview with Houston superintendent Terry Grier, who has run nine school districts over twenty-five years, Grier theorizes, "I think some principals accept mediocrity because they don't want to go through the battle with the teachers' union or through the process of aggressively recruiting others." *There is a need to apply pressure on those who lack the courage to combat mediocrity.*

The term "pressure" is an emotionally charged concept within education. Fullan (2009) expands our thinking about the value of using pressure to motivate activity:

> The opposite of pressure is not no pressure. No pressure is complacency. No pressure is inertia's other best friend. . . . A focused sense of urgency gets people's attention; partnership and peer learning increase support, but also pressure from successful cases (if it is done in circumstances similar to ours); *transparency of data makes it even more evident who is successful and who is not.*

Fullan goes on to explain differences in positive and negative pressure, but a critical point is that pressure is not an either/or situation. Pressure can be very motivational and is enhanced by transparency: "It exposes not only results, but practices that produce results. It generates specific, precise, visually clear images of what works. It is accessible for all as *it takes all excuses off the table.*"

Incorporating objective data, such as student achievement on tests, applies additional pressure to raise teaching standards, but this method is not without its own hiccups. Such a program is still managed by people within the system, and can still be politically manipulated as evidenced by Anderson's report on one American county. Cut scores from test data used in evaluating teachers were set relatively high, but when only 78 percent of teachers were deemed "highly effective" or "effective," and w*hen they saw how lenient other neighboring districts in the county were,* they *reset* them much lower. Ultimately, 99.4 percent of teachers were rated "effective" or "highly effective."

A NEW FRONTIER IN TEACHER EVALUATION

Utilizing test scores in teacher evaluation systems is a relatively new endeavor. There will be problems not unlike those evident in how teachers assess students. *Misuse by some does not mean disuse generally.* There is more promise for fairness than what occurs when educational systems rely exclusively on the teachers' assessments of students' work in the classroom.

The significant degree of grade inflation that occurs when a teacher-student relationship influences assessments is a concern.

Some school systems frequently rely on external tests for generating marks used in decisions regarding scholarships and placements into prestigious universities. This methodology requires a consistent application of cut scores so that there is adherence to standards and fixed goal posts are not moving. Students may feel disadvantaged by not being able to influence marks through strategies in compliant behavior, but they benefit from having their learning assessed by an unbiased process. *Fairness to students* is enhanced.

Undoubtedly teacher unions will continue to denounce use of test scores in evaluating teachers. Introducing measures of empirical data decreases their opportunity to challenge ratings of poor performance in the classroom. Even though teaching processes observed by evaluators continue to comprise most of the final evaluation, there finally is a shift underway to consider learner outcomes. *Learning is no longer the sole responsibility of the student.* This shift, by itself, is a major revolution in education.

However, this revolution presents a problem for politicians. Their electability is threatened when they adopt an allegiance to students, *who cannot vote*. In New York State, for example, complaints quickly surfaced in 2014 when results on the new Common Core tests were released. In New York City, 26 percent of students in third through eighth grade passed the tests in English and 30 percent passed in mathematics. These new tests emphasized deep analysis and creative problem solving rather than the traditional approach of short answers and memorization. In the previous year, when the old tests were used, 47 percent of city students passed in English and 60 percent in mathematics.

Across the state, the downward shift was similar: 31 percent of students passed the exams in reading and mathematics, compared with 55 percent in reading and 65 percent in mathematics the previous year. These poor results were chilling news for politicians, who sanctioned the previous testing program where standards were being systematically reduced in order to qualify for improvement grants under the No Child Left Behind legislation.

Their deception exposed, politicians reacted immediately as leaders of both political parties in the New York State Legislature called on the state to back away from plans to use those exams to grade teacher performance. A news report in the *New York Times* on February 4, 2014, captured the political paranoia:

> In synchronized statements, Democratic leaders of the State Assembly joined Republicans in the State Senate to propose that the tests, which are aligned with the new curriculum standards known as the Common Core, be excluded, for now, from the state's new teacher evaluation system, which Gov. Andrew M. Cuomo signed into law in 2012.

The proposal will involve altering the law, which requires that the state test results be used for at least 20 percent of a teacher's evaluation. Other factors, like principals' observations and locally designed tests, make up the bulk of the grade. Teachers who earn the lowest mark—"ineffective"—two years in a row are at risk of losing their jobs.

The change would require backtracking on one of the governor's earliest legislative victories. But it also could give him an antidote to mounting complaints over the Common Core in a re-election year. Mr. Cuomo has already said he would name a panel to recommend changes to what he called a "flawed" rollout of the Common Core.

The key phrase in this article—"an antidote to mounting complaints over the Common Core in a re-election year"— demonstrates succinctly how *politicians perpetuate unfairness to their students in deference to teachers and their unions.* Too frequently an election causes politicians to subjugate education's clients' best interests simply because they are not on the voters' lists. For a period of time, the New York school system will revert to an evaluation system based on principals' evaluations, as deeply flawed as this process is.

This hesitation to proceed with the most challenging aspect of attaching consequences with performance as required in the US national effort of the Race to the Top initiative provides a clear example regarding how politicians align with their most powerful special interest group: teachers' unions. New York is a Democrat state, and teacher unions support Democrat candidates overwhelmingly. Wikipedia reports,

> Based on required filings with the federal government, it is estimated that between 1990 and 2002 eighty percent of the NEA's substantial political contributions went to Democratic Party candidates. Although this has been questioned as being out of balance with the more diverse political views of the broader membership, the NEA maintains that it bases support for candidates primarily on the organization's interpretation of candidates' support for public education and educators. Every Presidential candidate endorsed by NEA must be approved by majority vote among the members themselves at NEA's annual Representative Assembly.

Similar delays in incorporating student achievement on system tests into teacher evaluations are reported in 2014 for California and Iowa. Both states voted Democrat in the 2012 presidential election. *It is not an overstatement to say that the power of teachers' unions is persuasive and pervasive.*

Nevertheless, progress in attaching higher levels of accountability to teachers for improving student achievement is being made across the United States. One publication, *The National Council on Teacher Quality,* reports a successful trend using data for years 2009, 2011, and 2013:

- Requiring *annual* evaluation of all teachers: fifteen, twenty-five, and twenty-eight states.
- Student achievement is the *preponderant* criterion in teacher evaluation: four, thirteen, and twenty states.
- Evidence of effectiveness is the basis of teacher *tenure* decisions: zero, eight, and nineteen states.

Making use of empirical data is a critical aspect for reforming valid and reliable teacher evaluations; however, there remains a requirement to resolve the issue that coaches should not also be the evaluator. School administrators, wanting to achieve the highest level of teamwork possible, risk many negative consequences when they provide staff with multilevel evaluations (e.g., five-point scale) including one that severs the relationship.

During a discussion on this issue with superintendents, one told of his experience with principals. The school district had a contractual provision that teachers on the substitute list held seniority over nonhired applicants if they produced a "satisfactory" evaluation on fourteen out of seventeen elements of instruction on two consecutive substituting placements involving three or more days. His district was surrounded by other districts and many of the teachers in the substitute pool accepted assignments in all of them but were routinely overlooked when they were hiring.

This superintendent was concerned that principals would have very low expectations during their evaluations of these long-term substitutes. These principals were anxious that the teachers' union would target them, and the superintendent's concerns materialized, as virtually all evaluations met the minimum requirement for hiring. The superintendent implemented a check-and-balance approach by designating a district officer to conduct all second assessments after the substitute teacher had received the initial qualifying report.

Many substitute teachers qualified for the minimal standard and the district was forced to hire them even though outstanding teachers from other places or from universities were bypassed. The critical point, however, is that the district officer shielded the district from having to hire many teachers who were not highly talented but were able to obtain satisfactory reports from principals who might never have them placed in their school.

This superintendent's experience reiterates how teacher evaluations should be undertaken by someone external to the school. District staff want to be known as instructional leaders and including *teacher evaluations* as part of their job description is a higher-order activity. Their involvement not only raises the profile of district staff but it also signals the school district's commitment for having highly competent teachers. Incorporating this responsibility cannot be perceived as an add-on but a basic leadership function required of all administrators.

Earlier in this book, Edmonton school district's success was heralded for improving student achievement the longer they were enrolled within the district. A follow-up conversation with the superintendent revealed his commitment to instructional leadership. During his four-year tenure, 7500 classrooms were visited after discussions with the principal when he asked three basic questions: What will we see? What won't we see? What is your coaching plan for this teacher?

A school district with 80,000 students can easily distract central office staff from their instructional leadership functions by making "administrivia" their primary mandate. These visits consumed a significant amount of time but ensuring that schools were improving was this superintendent's central purpose. His slogan, "Failure is not an option," was a driving force and, *when a school was not improving, this superintendent intervened in the school's autonomy by designing the school's professional development program.*

Parents were the beneficiaries of this passionate leadership *because their children were winning.* Some people may espouse that a politically correct posture is to have school staff prepare their professional development so that ownership is enhanced. Instead this superintendent believed there is a sense of urgency so that some students are not disadvantaged to accommodate politically correct activity. Years later on March 1, 2010, US president Obama made a related statement to the US Chamber of Commerce, "Our kids only get one chance at an education and we need to get it right."

Principals may be well-intentioned people but their track record in evaluating teachers is abysmal. Mutually beneficial back scratching dominates our schools' politically correct culture where people other than students occupy the pyramidal pinnacle. Teacher evaluation is so important that it must be the focus of all administrators selected for leadership functions in the school district offices. Achieving excellent teacher services for our children requires a two-pronged approach. The principal's work should be focused on *developing teacher talent* while the district office should be responsible for providing an arms-length function of *evaluating teacher performance.*

KEY POINTS

- We cannot trust even well-intentioned people if they are not good at what they are doing.
- Education is plagued by a model that places the school principal in a dual role as a teacher/coach and evaluator.
- Relationships cause grade inflation to be pandemic in education including when principals evaluate their teachers.

- Staff evaluation processes produce a culture dominated by mutual "back scratching."
- Use of empirical evidence in staff evaluations is changing the status quo; however, many politicians wilt in their commitments to incorporate empirical data into staff evaluations.
- Teacher evaluations should be conducted by someone outside of the school, which provides excellent opportunity for district staff to engage in instructional leadership.

Chapter 7

Birth Rather Than Worth Matters Too Much

Children are a nation's most valuable resource. They enter the world helpless, totally dependent on nurturing parents and other adults. Most spend a substantial portion of their childhood in a government-sponsored education system. Even when they enter their "first right of passage" as school children, they remain essentially ignorant of the hopes and dreams adults have for them. Once in school they are surrounded by people who espouse commitment to helping them achieve their potential.

Most progress through twelve years of primary and secondary education with relatively few setbacks and go on to experience varying levels of success in their personal and professional lives. But a considerable number do not, and their story is largely untold and misunderstood. With so many resources and so much attention devoted to them, it seems inconceivable and even unconscionable that such a large group begins to experience difficulties and even *failure as soon as they begin formal schooling*. Are there policies and practices in place that can be changed to remove aspects of schooling that are unfair?

It is even more distressing to know that difficulties attributable to the school system frequently have a lifelong negative impact on a child. Apprehensions about these difficulties and enduring consequences lead to tensions between home and school as the adults involved endeavor to assess each child's potential and determine what educational, compensatory programming is required to address gaps between expectations and achievement.

Old, seemingly imponderable questions surface again, often in heated debate. "Isn't the system at fault?" "Can't we change schooling practices to ensure a far higher rate of success?" "Shouldn't we spend more to compensate for deficiencies in a child's home environment?" Are there answers to these questions that are reasonable and readily implemented? The questions even go so far as to tap foundational social issues, such as the appropriate age for starting school.

SIGNIFICANT GAPS EXIST IN STUDENT ACHIEVEMENT

With a societal expectation that participation in the education system should be universal, the range in potential for academic success within an age cohort of students is significant. Tension emerges when schools seek to implement programs to address the differences in potential that surface, and debates about the fairness of opportunity erupt as gaps in success develop between children in a particular grade cohort.

All sides in the debate share a conviction that *schools should address those gaps in a child's success that can be attributed to them.* Social conscience dictates that decision-makers need to assess the potential impact of their decisions on children and make informed adjustments that eliminate as many barriers to success as possible. Factors, such as tradition, ignorance, entitlement, and change fatigue, frequently result in resistance or at least reticence to adapt in the face of persuasive evidence.

This chapter argues that our love for children and our reliance on them for the future well-being of the country and world means that those *forces and factors aligned against change must be respectfully and firmly challenged.* Initiative for change typically starts with leadership and it is axiomatic that all leadership makes a difference: *the issue is whether that difference is positive or negative.* In other words, *leadership is not a neutral force in the change equation.*

Until recently there has been insufficient data to convince an apathetic public about the urgent need for change. It has also meant that educational leaders, who are generally aware of the problem, have done little to level the "playing field" in education for a significant percent of the student population. So marked has this lethargy been that it raises a question as to whether or not our society really values children as its most important resource. Rather than change how schools function, the educator's response has been to move children along using a practice known as "social promotion."

As a result, a substantial proportion of our children leave their first career with skill and knowledge deficiencies, along with an inaccurate view of themselves and the world in which they live. *In short, they leave disadvantaged.* This does not stop our educational leaders from professing, at least in public, their commitment to student well-being. Responsible queries result in defensive language from within the educational system about the lack of resources available to address limitless needs.

A politically correct response typifies a need to overcome the wide range of educational success evident in our young children. Throwing more money at identified problems is the government's seemingly common response; however, removing children from their homes at earlier ages is increasingly common. Earlier institutionalization is now the politically correct response. Many European nations already institutionalize children as early as age two.

In North America, system leaders are increasingly implementing full-day kindergarten programs and even going younger.

There is an option for resisting these tendencies to spend more and institutionalize sooner. During presentations regarding this option, some people find it reprehensible to suggest that substantial savings actually occur by implementing a change in how the school system is organized. Their propensity for using increases in funding to measure performance made objectionable any initiative that decreased spending. *A suggestion to delay school entry and narrow the grouping's age range was too simple a solution.*

To a six-year-old child, one year is a monumental period of time because it represents approximately 16 percent of their lives. Physically, during a twelve-month window, they will likely experience phenomenal size changes in their clothing and footwear. These physical adjustments, which are recognized as a normal part of life, have to be accommodated in the family budget. Every parent understands this reality and makes financial plans to adjust to a substantial increase in family expenses.

There are no long-term negative effects of undergoing changes in physical development at different stages in life unless, as Gladwell records in his research, the child aspires to a career that relies on physical ability, such as is required of professional athletes (Gladwell, 2008). Participation in an elite athletic endeavor is related to variances in physical development but, for the vast majority of children, the reality of a twelve-month spread in physical development is merely a bump in their road to adulthood. Outside of the sports arena, few careers require extraordinary foot speed, height, arm reach, or physical strength.

When the focus shifts to the intellectual domain, every child is potentially affected because every child attends school where the primary responsibility is the development of intellectual capacity. A child's development in the social, emotional, physical, and spiritual domains is the primary responsibility of the home, although the school shares some supportive responsibility in these important areas. *Developmental delays in the intellectual domain are a serious concern for educators, because it is recognized that this domain is the school's primary responsibility.*

Parents express great pride and pleasure when their child is able to write their own name, count to one hundred, repeat in order the letters of the alphabet, read through a particular reader, and so on. Teachers feel the subtle and not so subtle pressure of curricular expectations or standards that are identified as learning outcomes for students in the various grades. *Children are not immune to the emotional effects of this focus on their intellectual development because they sense the pressure adults are feeling.*

This pressure is not inconsequential. In fact, our society imposes a great deal of pressure on children to succeed intellectually: it is promoted as the most important key to future success. As a consequence of this expectation, a child's self-esteem is closely associated with academic success. For the child, this pressure of academic success has considerable impact on self-esteem. Expressions such as "success breeds success" and "self-fulfilled prophecy" are not simply clichés: they have meaning and import for children in classrooms and both are tied to the issue of *relative-age effect* and annual, *single-date entry*.

Early success breeds confidence in a child, who will then feel able to attempt the learning challenges set out in a curriculum that is generally designed to have most students succeed. On the other hand, lack of success leads to self-doubt and self-imposed fear about tackling any new learning when failure seems probable. "I can't do this" soon becomes the student's mantra leading to negative thought patterns of self-doubt and inadequacy, especially in relationship to peers.

The emotional well-being of a child is absolutely critical because only *one in eight Grade 1 students, who falls behind the peer group, is able to catch up later* (Juel et al., 2003). Therefore, success in Grade 1 is so critical for the child's well-being that those who make policy in our society must consider all options that offer the promise of improving a child's rate of success. If, as educators and politicians are so fond of saying, "Children are our country's most valuable resource," are we really doing all we can to accommodate the nurturing of this resource?

Unfortunately, the answer is, "No!" As already stated, a year to a Grade 1 student represents 16 percent of their very brief lifetime. Substantial variances in intellectual development are readily apparent when two children sit in a classroom next to each other and the progress of one learner, who has lived approximately *eighty months*, is compared with another who has lived only *sixty-eight months*.

Many in the school establishment will rise in righteous indignation at any suggestion that schools are competitive environments where students are compared to each other. Curriculum is written in such a way as to describe educational progress in terms of standards, not rank in a class. The child, however, does not understand this subtlety, nor do many parents. *The child merely notices that their progress and success is not yet at the same level as others in the classroom.* The result is negative self-esteem even though they are pursuing a standard. The parent, too, notices that a number of their child's peers have skills that their child does not have.

Extensive research across the world demonstrates how disadvantaged are children born in the *latter half of the school year's registration window* (Dueck, 2013). *Their level of achievement on standardized tests is literally related with their birth month.* Data from an extensive study over a six-year period with more than 250,000 Grade 3 students reveals the significance of the relative-age effect in an annual, single-date entry system on student achievement (see figure 7.1).

If it is true that a "picture is worth a thousand words," then this picture should be sufficient reason to challenge lawmakers about continuing their current practices. The results of this carefully crafted and monitored study shows a steady drop in achievement in the April–December age groups. It provides incontrovertible evidence *that the majority of students are not maximizing their learning potential in the current twelve-month cohort system.*

The figure shows language arts test results by way of mean achievement scores for all students with a birthday in a particular month of the school year. Students born in March have the highest test scores and results for subsequent months show a gradual, but statistically significant, decline. *Simply stated, older students' achievement is higher than that of younger ones.*

Whereas a small majority of school districts in this region have a school registration from January 1–December 31, many school districts extend the cut-off to the end of the *second February* to entice parents to their district. As the bar graph reaches the right side of the chart, the achievement level of students born in the *second January and February* fits the pattern that younger students achieve at lower levels than older students.

Test results for these second January and February birth-month students makes apparent the *foolishness of school districts permitting children born in these months to enroll in school when they are as young as five-and-a-half years old.* It is an unconscionable abuse of authority for leaders to admit groups of students into a class when it is known their chances of success are significantly reduced.

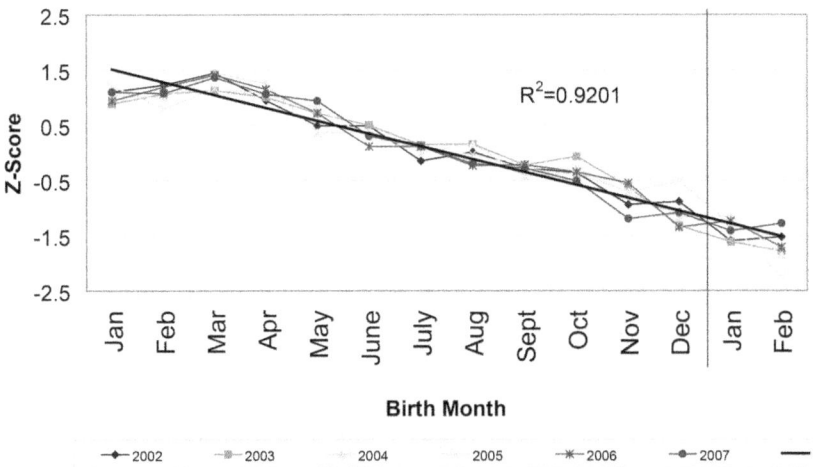

Figure 7.1 Grade Three Test Scores by Birth Month

One of the interesting, consistent features of figure 7.1 is the success of students born in March. Based on the rest of the evidence, this is counterintuitive. Students born in March are not the oldest but they demonstrate the highest level of achievement. January and February birth-month students are older but demonstrate a slightly lower level of achievement. *The tragedy within this graphic is that there are many students who started school in their second January or February, but were too immature to achieve success. They were subsequently retained for a year, and then wrote the Grade 3 tests with the cohort of students born during the regular January to December registration period.*

Even though these students spent *an additional year in school and were now with their age cohort,* their achievement on the test was not as high as that of their same-age peers who started school when they were six years old. In other words, the immature, retained learner pulled down the January and February results because the *damage to their self-esteem mitigated some of the success* they would have experienced had they waited to start school with their age cohort. In effect, *the education system penalized these younger students.*

Our study then followed a one-year cohort of 45,000 students who started kindergarten in 1996. By the end of that school year, virtually all children born between January 1 and May 31 progressed to Grade 1 next September. The percentage of students retained increased to 1 percent in June to an astonishing 20 percent for December birthdates. In total, 2.9 percent of the kindergarten cohort for 1996 was retained and the reduced cohort of students entering Grade 1 in 1997 was followed for the next nine years until entering senior high school.

Figure 7.2 depicts the retentions by birth month during each grade by the time the cohort completed Grade 9. Students who entered kindergarten with a January/February birthdate, but as four-year-olds, experienced high retention rates. Children born from January 1 to May 31 and were six-years-old when they began Grade 1 experienced a retention rate of less than 10 percent by the *end of Grade 9*. Children born in the second half of the registration year as well as those born in the second January and February—but progressed into Grade 1 after one year in kindergarten—experienced retention rates up to 30 percent.

Examining the entire cohort of students in kindergarten during the 1996/1997 school year, retentions by 2006 totaled 16.9 percent (2.9 percent in kindergarten + 13.8 percent in Grades 1–9) or approximately *one in six students*. This analysis of achievement data by birth month reveals how rules related to school registration disadvantage a significant percentage of our students.

At this point, it is appropriate to make a quip that an *important aspect of parenting is knowing when to become pregnant*. Wise prospective parents, *who realize that the school system experiences difficulty in changing its ways,* will undertake family planning so that children are born in the *first three months* of the school year's *registration window*.

Figure 7.2   Student Retentions after Grade Nine by Birth Month

SCHOOLS PENALIZE ACADEMICALLY STRONG STUDENTS

Unfortunately, there are also negative implications for parents wanting to provide their children with this advantage. The school system is committed to *helping weak students* to such a degree that it responds with what Michael Fullan called a "moral imperative" to help all who are needy and disadvantaged (Fullan, 2003). Educators commit themselves to raising the achievement levels of all who are struggling in their class. Because the more capable students are not in need of special attention, their needs become secondary, which in turn consigns them to an achievement level below their full potential.

In this relative-age-effect discussion there is little understanding of this "glass ceiling" effect evident in the literature to date. However, in 2011, a study in the United States (Xiang et al.) emerged with the rather catchy promotional statement on the front cover: "The first U.S. study to examine the performance of America's highest-achieving children over time at the individual-student level." Contained within the report was an even more probing question which asked, "Do high flyers maintain their altitude?"

This timely report tracked the outcomes of American students who were high flyers initially, but who "fell off the bus" several years later. Specifically, students were tracked by achievement groups with the first group comprising high flyers in Grade 3 and then assessed in Grade 8. The researchers tracked a second group from Grades 6 through 10.

This national report indicated the percentage of students who "lost altitude" from high flyer status between Grade 3 and Grade 8. In mathematics, 43 percent of students descended, while in reading it was 44 percent. In the Grades 6 through 10 study, 30 percent descended in mathematics and 48 percent descended in reading. The report concluded that "descenders" dropped from the 94th percentile to the 77th percentile or from the top 10 percent of their grade to the top 30 percent. Chester Finn, whom Xiang quotes, stated:

> If America is to remain internationally competitive with other advanced nations, we need to maximize the potential of our top students. Yet many analysts worry that various policies and programs tend to level student achievement by focusing on the lowest-achieving students and ignoring, or worse, *driving resources away from our strongest students.*

Finn's warning and challenge are really an indictment of the social promotion/grade inflation/moral imperative philosophies of our day that inform and inspire decision-makers. No aspect of these well-meaning but errant ideas is more deleterious than the twelve-month, single-date entry cohort concept that *functions together in penalizing students but without being exposed to the unquestioning minds of an uninformed public.*

Figure 7.3 categorizes students born in March and the second February by their standardized test score in Grade 3. In effect, the age difference in the two groups is approximately twelve months, but what makes them particularly interesting is that they represent the highest and lowest points of achievement on the scale. Achievement levels are aggregated for the initial 0 to 29 percent range because numbers are relatively small, but the other students fell into categories created by deciles. The two bar lines represent "gains" in student achievement according to the two birth months.

Students in Grade 3 scoring in the 60 to 69 and 70 to 79 percent ranges in Grade 3 testing demonstrate approximately a 0 percent gain in achievement in Grade 9. In other words, these *students gained what was expected during the next six years of school*, and achieved in Grade 9 at the same level as they achieved in Grade 3. Essentially they acquired six years of learning in six years. This pattern represents satisfactory performance.

Students scoring less than 60 percent in Grade 3 recorded a "gain" for the average student. For example, students scoring in the 30 to 39 percent range in Grade 3 improved their average mark by approximately 17 percent. This may be a good news story because the schools' efforts at *improving low levels of student achievement were successful*. However, this happy conclusion needs to be nuanced: Is the gain sufficient? Is it what one would anticipate? Nevertheless, there was a gain!

Unfortunately, there is also a "loss" or decline for a particular group of students. Those with a Grade 3 mark in the nineties had their average

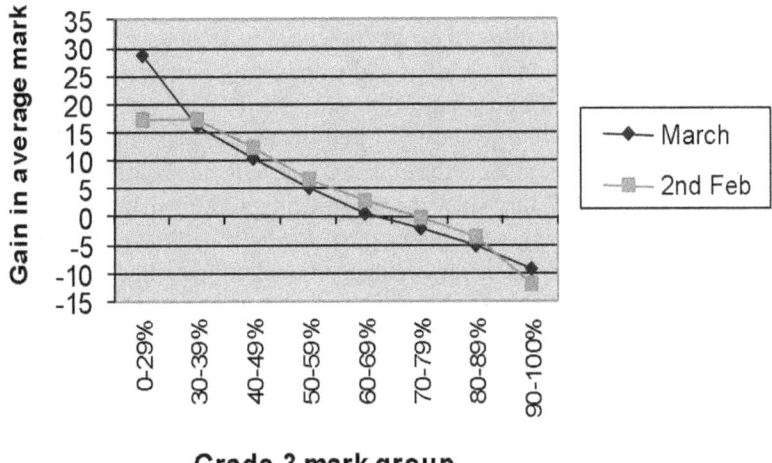

Grade 3 mark group

Figure 7.3 Gains by Grade Three Students Comparing March and Second February Births

Grade 9 mark *decline* by approximately 10 percent. Declining levels in student achievement were recorded for students in general who had achieved marks above 70 percent. *The schools' efforts toward improving achievement levels of low-performing students prevented high achievers from maintaining, much less improving, their success.*

Figure 7.3 is also very significant because it demonstrates that students born in the second February did *not gain* on those born in the first February despite having so much opportunity to do so. Therefore, despite all of the schools' efforts to bring these very young students up to grade level they *remained as far behind in Grade 9 as they were in Grade 3*. Again, birth-month data demonstrates long-term disadvantage for the younger students.

There was one exception to the pattern of gains and declines diverging for the two age groups. Student test scores in Grade 3 for the 0 to 29 percent range for both birth months demonstrated improved results in Grade 9 but the older students (March) improved to a greater extent. In other words, the intensive assistance the schools provided to achieve the moral imperative of helping the lower-achieving students was particularly successful with the older, more mature students.

The chart also provides an insight into the bigger issue of an important enrolment date for children. The gain or decline between any two birth months that were exactly six years apart, was virtually the same from Grade 3 to 9 in all scores that ranged from 30 to 100 percent. In other words, *younger students were unable to overcome the deficit they had when they enrolled.* Time did not ameliorate the negative impact, which began in the fall of the first year. Data from this chart alone should motivate school systems to caution parents about enrolling their young children at an early age.

Yes, there are exceptional children and extenuating circumstances, but the averages indicate that disadvantages are perpetuated for many years. This region during the period of this study required students to make major decisions about their high school courses at the end of Grade 9, that is before they entered high school. Once again this left younger students with their relatively lower achievement scores paying yet another price for their early start in school as they were relegated to lower stream courses in a school they had yet to attend. *Ultimately these lower stream courses limited students' access to universities.*

Figure 7.3, then, portrays some good news regarding future success by Grade 9 for the weaker Grade 3 students. However, many students were retained after Grade 3 and wrote the Grade 9 test while taking seven years instead of six to reach Grade 9. Therefore, some of the achievement gains occurring from Grade 3 to 9 for the lower-achieving students, when they were in Grade 3, can be attributed to the intellectual maturation gained in the additional year.

The central point is that efforts to achieve the imperative of improving achievement for the weaker students, who were mostly younger students, interfered with the achievement of stronger, mostly older students. This research and the study from the United States are the first studies to demonstrate an impact regarding relative-age effect on older and more capable students. *Unfortunately, the effect is negative.* It is also important to emphasize that these findings are about *generalizations and not rules*. Exceptions with specific students to these generalizations can occur but these studies portray a general problem within our school system.

During discussions with school administrators one explained the negativity of this moral imperative to focus on the weak students by stating succinctly, "We need to help kids at the top more because our leaders in society are mostly from the top. Instead we go to the 'drowners' first because that is where we have the sense of urgency." The argument is certainly not that the future "leaders," as the administrator put it, receive "more help" than the "drowners," but rather that all children receive the help they need to achieve their potential. The result of our current practice is a figurative "glass ceiling" for those with ability, *and it is unfair, unjust, and unwise.*

SEMESTERIZING ELEMENTARY SCHOOLS

There is a relatively simple solution to this two-pronged dilemma but it requires policy-makers to change their thinking from placing teachers on top of the education pyramid, which is the current politically correct response, to having students sit atop the throne. The model already exists in our schools and can be readily implemented with a slight but significant modification. *There is no need to maintain a school organization that is unfair to such a large percentage of our children.*

The two-semester year is in place with older students and incorporating this concept with our youngest children provides the structure for increasing fairness for all students. High schools use the semester by teaching a year's curriculum in one-half of the school year but meeting with their classes twice as often or long. They then teach the other courses in the second half of the school year and, again, twice as often or long.

The semester approach for students beginning their school career—that is, kindergarten or Grade 1—features a dual entry with a six-month range in birthdates for each semester. For example, children born between February 1 and July 31 begin their school year in September, while those born between August 1 and January 31 begin school in February. Splitting a one-year age range into two groups has a dramatic effect on student success.

Parents sometimes stumble over the concept of summer vacation for children who begin their schooling at the beginning of February. Going to school for ten months and then having summer vacation is so engrained in our lifestyle, even though it originated due to an agrarian society. The break does not have to occur at the end of a grade just like the Christmas break does not have to occur near the middle of a grade. Learning is continuous and there is no difference when breaks occur.

The significant advantage in this approach is that students do not begin kindergarten until age five or Grade 1 until age six. Readiness to learn is an important issue for learning and an advantage in this approach is that entry for very young children in the current approach is delayed by six months. Referring back to figure 7.1, student achievement in the lower half of the achievement scale is upgraded to the top half. They become high achievers because they are more mature. *Accommodating time to mature increases fairness for our children.*

A 50 percent reduced age range is the second prong in this approach. Students born seven to twelve months behind the oldest in the group are no longer in the same group and worrying that they are falling behind. *Self-esteem is no longer victimized to the extent this happens in our current structure.* Teachers benefit because the range in students' abilities is reduced and they are teaching more mature children.

The most dramatic reality comes from comparing the retention rates for students in the sixth and twelfth months. Retentions from kindergarten to Grade 9 for the sixth month were approximately 11 percent and for the twelfth month 30 percent. Dual entry has the effect of improving student achievement for this twelfth-month group to the equivalent of sixth-month students. *A 173 percent reduction in retentions for the last month in our existing structure would be unheralded.*

HUGE STUDENT GAINS WITH HUGE FINANCIAL SAVINGS

There are substantial savings from implementing dual entry beginning with one in effect for thirteen years until dual exit from Grade 12 occurs. The traditional entry into kindergarten (or Grade 1) features approximately one-half of the usual cohort until they begin in the "second semester" of the September 1–June 30 calendar. *This annual savings is approximately 2 percent annually for thirteen years* providing a two-pronged benefit: *higher achievement at less cost.*

Huge additional savings accompany the dual-entry concept. Student retention in the current single-date entry system is significant, and accommodating retained students for a longer period of time than the traditional twelve years requires *more teachers, classrooms, and support staff such as caretakers, secretaries, etc.* Recall *that one in six students was being retained an additional year in school* and that the significant majority of these were victims of the single-entry date system. *Dual entry greatly reduces the number of students requiring an additional year in school.*

Furthermore, much of the existing need for *costly remediation programs* is eliminated. In the existing annual single-date entry, the school system is attempting to achieve its *moral imperative* with so many students who are in need of remediation simply because of immaturity. Not only are there savings in remedial teachers but also in their support services such as school psychologists who, in focus groups, report that almost all clients were students born in the last quarter of the registration window.

The combined savings beyond the initial 2 percent for dual entry are difficult to calculate but can be several times this amount. Additional *capital savings* are also accrued from having fewer numbers of students spending an additional year in school. Fewer classrooms result in fewer schools and less costs associated with heating, lighting, and cleaning.

The data presented in this chapter guarantees a huge savings or re-deployment of the annual operating budget while achieving a significant boost in student achievement for students born in the second half of the registration period. *Governments can actually redeploy savings to other departments or services, or allow the school system to retain the savings and enhance services to students, or actually reduce taxes for its citizens.*

Not calculated, at this point, is the gain in student success that would occur to top-achieving students, *who would no longer be constrained in their intellectual development by the "glass ceiling effect" brought about by education's pursuit of the moral imperative.* Too many of our brightest and best students lose their motivation to excel in school when teachers are so focused on the needs of less mature students.

During a presentation to groups of parents on this concept, one parent responded with considerable cynicism. "A great idea but it will never happen," he said. "The school system is far too resistant to make this change even though it is relatively minor and saves a lot of money." Malcolm Gladwell (2008) expressed a similar frustration about societal tendencies with his summary:

> We could easily take control of the machinery of achievement . . . *but we don't*. And why? Because we cling to the idea that success is a simple function of individual merit and that the world into which we all grow up and the rules we choose to write as a society don't matter at all.

It is incomprehensible to think that the education system could purposely perpetuate unfair situations to a nation's most valuable resource. However, when a rule has been in place for so long—in this case centuries—it is difficult to replace it with an alternative. Peter Senge, renowned researcher on change and director of the Center for Organizational Learning at the MIT Sloan School of Management, once commented in an informal setting that *achieving change in education was more difficult than in any other profession.*

We can explain this in part by the fact that the relatively low level of accountability in education results in *little pressure from the stakeholders for change*. Therefore, since the school system finds it difficult to change, prospective parents need to plan for a birth month of their children so that these occur early in a school system's registration window. When schools resist change, parents must make changes to at least protect their child from this educational maleficence. The politically correct approach of throwing more money at the problem and institutionalizing children at a younger age are failing strategies.

EXPLORING THE FINNISH MODEL

A dual-entry concept counters the prevailing approach of institutionalizing children at an earlier age and placing children in learning groups where the age spread is twelve months and more. A significant component within this concept involves delaying a child's entry into schooling until they are approximately six years of age. Maturation is key for learning and this delay for younger students provides the opportunity for many to enhance their capacity for success.

Finland's success on international assessments has received worldwide scrutiny with little attention given to students' maturation levels. Their educational model actually delays formal schooling until age seven which is up to 1.5 years delayed from many North American school systems: a 27 percent delay of a child's life. Reviews of Finland's educational success frequently disregard some data that immediately raises eyebrows.

The chart in figure 7.4 compiled in 2005 by the Council of Ministers of Education in Canada (CMEC), demonstrates that Finland's students aged *seven through fourteen* spend the least amount of instructional time in school. Their student achievement results, however, were the highest in the world on the 2006 PISA tests. Indeed, Finland is consistently one of the highest-achieving education systems in the world.

The United States and Canada are missing from the chart because the data is difficult to gather in these two countries, which do not have a centralized national governance model in education. Therefore, there is not a consistent rule across the country about time spent in school or instructional hours. Overall, because these two countries are so similar in their educational structures and practices, children end up spending approximately as much time in school as France.

This graph certainly raises many questions but contains a powerful message about educating children. *Simply stated, less is more*! In Finland, children do *not* begin Grade 1 until the age of seven, whereas most countries in the world begin at least a year earlier, or even earlier.

As stated previously, intellectual maturation is significant in the early years of a child's life, and delaying the onset of formal schooling by a year provides the opportunity for many more children to reach the stage that is necessary

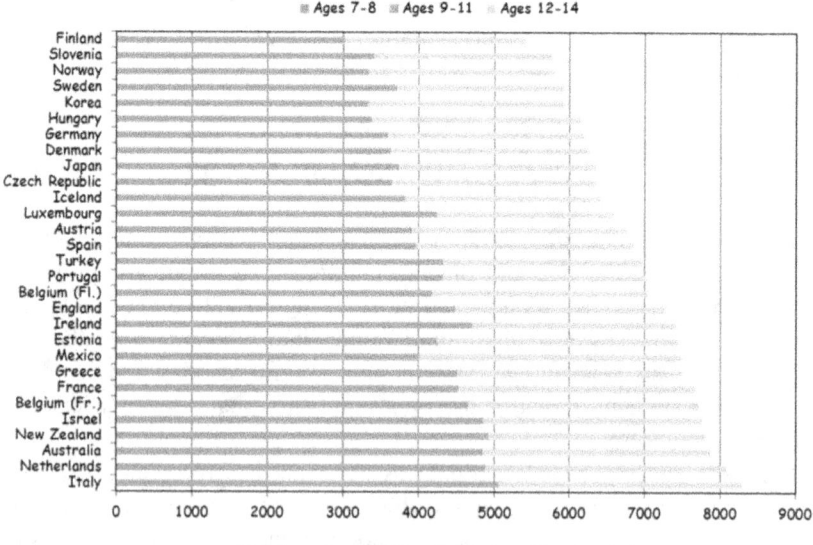

Figure 7.4 Time in School for Students in Selected Countries

for academic success. Since Finland and a few other countries in that region of the world do not begin formal schooling until age seven, the chart begins with that age in order to provide a consistent measure of instructional time in all countries for the period of time that children from all countries listed are in attendance.

If the chart began at age six, Finland's bar line would be considerably shorter than it already is relative to most of the other countries. Finland would add "zero" to the total, whereas most of the other countries would be adding close to 1,000 hours more instruction. Finland is truly one of the amazing enigmas in the ongoing debates about time on learning in educational reform.

Figure 7.4 tells a truly incredible story. Given the fact that the PISA tests are age-based tests and that all students writing the test are fifteen years old, it means that students in Finland will have had at least one year less of school than their peer group in most other countries. Eventually they go through twelve grades but they finish one year later than do students in most of the world. Their education system with a delayed entry results in a delayed exit.

In North America, students writing the PISA are usually in Grade 9 when the testing program is administered in March. Students in Finland are only in Grade 8; yet, their overall student achievement scores are at the highest level relative to the rest of the world. In some respects, their achievement level is simply profound yet profoundly simple. Their advantages with a unicultural society and commitment to education is, in this author's view, supported by a rule related to the age that students begin formal learning.

While Finns have only been in school for approximately 5,400 hours from age seven (i.e., including Grade 1) through age fourteen, French and North American students will have received approximately 7600 hours after Grade 1, that is, not counting the hours they had in Grade 1. Stated differently, students in France and North America spend approximately 40 percent more time in school from age seven through fourteen.

Including the additional year in Grade 1 that begins at the age of six, France and North America spend more than 50 percent greater time in school compared to their counterparts in Finland by the time they write the PISA tests at age fifteen. This is profound evidence that less can be more! Finland's strategy of delaying entry into formal learning for up to one year allows a larger percentage of students to begin formal learning when they are developmentally ready and more mature.

Such a rule makes much more sense in helping students achieve their potential than the many costly efforts of bringing students into preschool programs at earlier ages. It also reduces the need for costly expenditures for remediation programs and facilitates maximizing instructional time for students developmentally ready to learn. If the well-being of the child was not reason enough to adopt such a practice—and it is—the economic justification is clear: you get more "bang for the buck" if you delay children until they are mature enough to take advantage of the learning experience schools provide.

However, the cultural shift that would need to take place for age seven to be adopted in North America as the appropriate age to begin school is seemingly too great to be considered realistic. Reason, based on data, is irrelevant in the minds of many because this has been absent in education for too long. Added to this reticence to change, based on tradition and habit, is a public skepticism about research in the social sciences, a wish to have children in custodial care so that parents can get on with careers, and a desire to see children "race to the top" by queuing up early at the starting gate, that is, Grade 1.

In spite of all these societal obstacles, we must still make the case for consideration of the Finnish model. Their decision to delay entry until seven years of age has the effect of giving all children one more year to mature, thus closing the gap between January- and December-born children. Their approach effectively neutralizes the relative-age effect, because it ensures that almost all children are sufficiently mature to handle formal learning.

Even if their approach was not adopted by society as a whole, it should be offered as a reasonable alternative for schools and parents, thus giving our North American system a creative way to help more students achieve their potential. The end result would be a stronger, more equitable school system, which we could only see as a positive development. However, recognizing how dramatic such a shift will be in North American culture, this chapter proposes a dual approach where entry into school is delayed until age six and students are grouped in six-month cohorts.

KEY POINTS

- The range in potential for academic success within an age cohort of students is significant.
- The current system leaves many children disadvantaged but the politically correct approaches of throwing more money and institutionalizing children earlier are wrongheaded.
- Significantly more students born in the second half of a grade cohort are retained.
- Schools pay more attention to the educational needs of struggling students than with their gifted classmates.
- Reducing academic ability ranges in half provides huge benefits in both student achievement and financial savings.

- Politically correct attitudes prevent schools from instituting necessary changes and so parents should consider birth-month planning.
- Finland's education model, which has students begin school at age seven, demonstrates why readiness to learn—or maturation—is so important; however, it remains too dramatic a shift for North American culture.

Chapter 8

Teachers' Professional Development

North American education provides an excellent example of how *misplaced priorities can have deleterious consequences*. During a TED talk by Andreas Schleicher, who manages the PISA international testing program, he succinctly summarized an important dichotomy:

> One way you can spend money is by paying teachers well, and you can see Korea investing a lot in attracting the best people into the teaching profession. And Korea also invests into long school days, which drives up costs further. Last but not least, Koreans want their teachers not only to teach but also to develop. They invest in professional development and collaboration and many other things. All that costs money. How can Korea afford all of this? The answer is, *students in Korea learn in large classes.*

Staples, a reporter with the *Edmonton Journal*, reported on the 2012 release of PISA results including a follow-up interview with Schleicher:

> In Canada [and U.S.], a fair amount of its money has been *eaten up by reductions in class size*. It's been a very expensive move and *you can't reverse it*. Once you've gone that road, nobody is going to accept going back. It's very popular. Teachers like it. Parents like it. It's a very easy to do, very quick to do. But it's a *one-way road* because nobody is ever going to accept increases in class sizes either. It's very expensive and it drives out other possibilities. You can spend your money only once. If you spend it on a smaller class, you can no longer spend it on more professional development, on better working conditions, or on more pay and so on.

Schleicher's succinct summary provides politicians with a perspective that cannot be ignored. Disregarding research, while pandering to special interests in education, is costing taxpayers a great deal of money with little to show as a return on investment, but an entrenched expense that is almost impossible to reverse. *Once launched, initiatives become entitlements*, which turns out to be a politically correct culture.

SPENDING ON WORKING CONDITIONS HINDERS TEACHER DEVELOPMENT

Ensuring that our children are in classrooms with highly competent and effective teachers should be a priority for education administrators; however, this focus is hindered by yielding to *unions' demands for working conditions to the detriment of learning conditions*. Professional development for teachers is one of the areas that is floundering because the politically correct emphasis in education is on matters related to *teaching processes* rather than on *teaching outcomes*. Teachers' evaluations place too much emphasis on the processes observed during principals' visits to classrooms, *when this evaluator also serves as a coach*.

Professional development is more *haphazard* when teachers are not held accountable for improving student outcomes. Too frequently, professional development days are seen as a "holiday" from students or an opportunity to travel to a fancy hotel in a warm winter climate with expenses paid by tax dollars. Conferences have little accountability and sessions frequently begin with most attendees present but they lose many teachers out the back door part way through.

Darling-Hammond et al. (2009) concluded that districts should recognize how the problem is not about participation in professional development; rather, it is that, on the whole, the majority of the professional development they do participate in is *ineffective*. More than 90 percent of teachers reported having participated in professional development in the past year, but the majority also reported that it was *not* useful. This level of dissatisfaction is because most development happens in a workshop-style model which research shows *has little to no impact on student learning or teacher practice*.

In another major review, Yoon et al. (2007) reported that one-time workshops are the most prevalent model for delivering professional development; yet, workshops have an abysmal track record for changing teacher practice and improving student achievement. This report finds that when teachers actually receive substantial professional development—an average of forty-nine hours in their nine studies—their increased expertise can boost their students' achievement by 21 percentile points.

These researchers found that only lengthy and intensive professional development programs impacted student achievement. Programs that were less than fourteen hours (like the one-shot workshops commonly held in schools) had no effect on student achievement. Not only did these workshops fail to increase student learning, they did *not* even change teaching practices. When the training merely described a skill to teachers, as traditional workshops do, it was found that only 10 percent of teachers could transfer the skill to practice.

A superintendent concurred with this observation after holding a two-day workshop for all teachers on how to use cooperative learning in the classroom. During the following two years he visited 2,000 classrooms in his district and never observed employment of cooperative learning techniques. Even though these training sessions were conducted by acclaimed practitioners, the initiative failed to become a common practice because follow-through within the school did not occur.

These studies are not particularly earth shaking because anecdotal evidence confirms how widespread discontent is regarding the value of much of education's professional development. A difficulty in discussing this problem lies in how quickly educators accuse someone of "teacher bashing" by questioning the value of days *when schools are closed to students* so that teachers can hold professional development activity. While educators readily respond to studies such as the aforementioned, there is a perception that public criticism is politically incorrect.

This chapter's focus is about changing the laissez faire culture surrounding professional development to an environment where accountability is high. Not only should teachers be motivated to participate but they should also have high expectations that their specific needs will be addressed. In the end, they should see evidence that their teaching talent has improved because their students' learning is at the higher levels of achievement.

Jensen et al. (2016) undertook a worldwide review of professional development and reinforce this key issue:

> Ultimately, the system and its policy settings are all about student learning. Professional learning is seen as only being effective if it increases student learning. A teacher or a school leader will therefore never be recognised as good at professional *learning if they are ineffective at raising the performance of their students.*

Inputs, such as teaching processes used in the classroom, are the elements most frequently used in teacher evaluations. A concerted effort to incorporate outcomes from students' standardized test scores is occurring across the United States; however, such a focus in Canada, where teachers' unions hold a strong grip on politicians, remains in the politically *incorrect* realm. Improvement in test scores, where individual student achievement can be tracked annually, is a fundamentally sound approach in assessing teacher performance, and how teachers apply their professional development can be measured by their students' improvement on standardized tests.

PROFESSIONALIZING PROFESSIONAL DEVELOPMENT

A focus on student outcomes in teacher evaluations will change the laissez faire culture surrounding professional development. More strategies are necessary, however, to increase accountability during professional development activities so that return on investment is increased and the public can be assured that children benefit from days when schools shutter their doors to students.

Major conferences featuring recognized experts are frequently scheduled during the school year in resort areas across the United States. Expectations for participating teachers using public funds should require considerable payback to their school district for this privilege. Their application should include a commitment to provide several opportunities to present the contents of these conference sessions to district colleagues for their own distributed learning. Teaching others enhances their own skill and commitment for employing new teaching skills within their classroom.

This applicant should also provide a brief evaluation for each session attended, which includes information that will be helpful to others. These evaluations should include a rating on the presentation as well as who will find value in its content. Summary notes about the session increases accountability and also provides the participant with immediate opportunity to organize thoughts about how the session is transferrable into their own setting.

School district workshops should also conclude with an evaluation of the session and its presenter, which are kept on file by the district administrator responsible for staff development. The integrity of this approach is greatly increased when these evaluations are distributed and collected by someone other than the presenter. These assessments not only provide constructive feedback to the presenter but also determine future value for repeating the session. Accountability activities such as these can produce a consolidated evaluation, which is incorporated into the school district's report card.

At the individual staff level, personal professional development should incorporate two strategies. First and foremost, identifying annual individual goals requires introspection and thoughtful planning for the year's activities and a meaningful discussion with each person's supervisor. The critical component within the plan is the assessments individuals plan to use for determining success at the end of the year. It is insufficient to measure the goal using the word "completed." More thoughtful accountability will provide assessments that can quantify the degree to which goals are achieved.

PERSONALIZING PROFESSIONAL DEVELOPMENT

Every teacher has the capacity to provide professional development albeit at a more personal level. Working with a large group may create too much anxiety; however, a one-to-one activity is reasonable and should be associated with the process of setting annual, personal goals. Committing to peer observation with colleagues is an inexpensive approach that benefits teachers through observing colleagues within the same school with minimal cost and anxiety. Freeing teachers for these observations can be arranged by using preparation times, where these are available, or by coordinating scheduled observations across several classes using a substitute teacher.

For teachers, these observations entail pairing with a colleague for several scheduled classroom visits during a three- to four-month period. Each observation is followed by a two-way discussion in which the observer can ask questions and comment on topics about which the observed teacher may have wanted feedback. This is a dialogue in which professionals discuss issues from each perspective and one that engages both participants' philosophies about effective teaching strategies.

Beyond these observations nothing is formalized in writing; however, a three-way conversation including the school principal or assistant principal concludes the cycle. *This aspect provides the necessary accountability for ensuring that program objectives for professional development are addressed.* The discussion also concludes without any written records and provides each of the two teachers with the opportunity to summarize learnings acquired during the experience.

A similar process while developing personal goals occurs for school principals who "shadow" each other on several occasions. Their reviews also conclude without formal record keeping and their wrap-up for ensuring accountability is conducted with a district officer who supervises at least one of the participants.

Finally, ownership for the professional development agenda is desirable for achieving commitment and follow-through. Therefore, planning this agenda is usually the purview of each school and school district; however, accountability for improving student outcomes remains the driving force. When the school's report card demonstrates declining outcomes, good intentions are insufficient and the school district is obligated to intervene.

In an example referenced earlier, the Edmonton Public Schools' superintendent reviewed school outcomes and, if the data collection system was not producing satisfactory improvement, *the school's autonomy was reduced.* This superintendent recognized his responsibility as well as his motto that "failure is not an option" and he assumed responsibility for designing the schools' professional development program. School staff may find this intrusion to be politically incorrect; however, the "buck stops" with the superintendent who must ensure that students are atop education's pyramidal pinnacle.

Jensen et al. (2016) express a similar conclusion based on their observations of Shanghai's school system, the highest performer on PISA tests:

> The first [consequence for low performance] is that the school's autonomy is reduced. Normally, about 50% of a teacher's professional learning is determined by the school: if evaluations show that the school's professional learning is not up to standard, this could be reduced to 10%. *District level officials and those charged with helping schools will take over professional learning until the school considerably improves.*

Concluding this chapter requires a reminder that billions of dollars across North America are spent on teacher professional development but that researchers indicate too little return on investment. The laissez-faire environment in education regarding noninstructional days requires high levels of accountability so that taxpayers have evidence that their financial contribution is providing better educational services. Professional development days need to be more than just a holiday away from students when teachers can enjoy having lunch with acquaintances and stays in wonderful hotels at taxpayers' expense.

KEY POINTS

- Disregarding research, while pandering to special interests in education, is costing taxpayers a great deal of money with little to show as a return on investment, but an entrenched expense that is almost impossible to reverse.
- Teachers express little value for current approaches to professional development.
- Laissez faire attitudes toward professional development can be overcome by instituting accountability in numerous approaches.
- Eventually professional development must improve student outcomes or, if this improvement is not occurring, have the school's autonomy curtailed.

Chapter 9

Reducing Administration Costs

Bringing about change in education is difficult because the stakes are so low. We hold accountable that which is valued and the accountability bar in education is quite minimal. Most workers enjoy a job for life, assessments for both students and staff are highly inflated, most parents are held captive within their local school boundaries, and, particularly in the United States, spending on education is high without commensurate outcomes. Wasted spending is particularly evident in school district administrations where the number of districts is unreasonably high.

Models from the agrarian roots of our society need to be reconsidered in our present era of instant communication and rapid travel. Isolated communities across the United States are few and the horse-and-buggy era has long since passed. Organizational patterns from a century ago are unrealistic but frequently maintained because district administrators and school trustees are influential in any consultation regarding amalgamation. Their *obvious bias* toward instituting efficiencies at their expense is disregarded.

Return on investment, which is poor in the American school system, should be an important consideration in this discussion that proposes a dramatic reduction in the number of school districts across the United States. Local control is the countering argument in this debate; however, it is no longer as applicable because state offices now determine curricula and accountability.

Layton (2016) reported on how Republican governors already are diminishing local control by having their state takeover poor-performing school districts:

> Governors in Michigan, Arkansas, Nevada, Wisconsin, Georgia, Ohio and elsewhere—mostly Republican leaders who otherwise champion local control in their fights with the federal government—say they are intervening in cases of

chronic academic or financial failure. *They say they have a moral obligation to act when it is clear that local efforts haven't led to improvement.*

Undoubtedly these takeovers still require central offices and administrators and are intended to achieve better outcomes, but without pursuing administrative efficiencies through amalgamation.

A significant consideration pertains to the need for states to continue operating with as many small education authorities or school districts as are now in place. Amalgamating school districts is aimed at increasing efficiency by removing some of the administrative functions and releasing these savings for the purposes of reducing taxes or introducing educational reforms. In 2016 for example, the State of Kansas considered amalgamating districts with fewer than 10,000 students, which would reduce the number of districts from 286 to 132 and *save taxpayers $173 M over ten years* (Tobias, 2016).

The debate regarding wasted administrative costs is easier to understand by comparing the United States and Canada:

- US population is *nine times larger* than Canada.
- Canada is slightly larger in square miles but much of Canada is relatively *uninhabitable*.
- Canada has approximately 460 school districts; the United States has 13,506 (2002 US Census Bureau statistic).
- The ratio of US districts compared to Canada is 29:1.
- The ratio of US districts compared to Canada based on per capita is *slightly more than 3:1*.

While the United States has more than three times as many school districts per person, Canada's performance on international tests, such as PISA, greatly and consistently exceeds that of American schools. For example, scores for the 2012 PISA results were:

- Mathematics: Canada 518; the United States 481
- Reading: Canada 523; the United States 498
- Science: Canada 525; the United States 497

The school system's performance based on student outcomes should be the primary focus when determining optimal district size. The Canadian province of Alberta has two school districts (Calgary and Edmonton) with a substantially larger enrolment than other districts. Calgary, which hovered near 100,000 students for many years, had average results in provincial testing in 1998. The superintendent sent a message to everyone in the district with a public pronouncement that the district would pay attention to these test results in the future. Eight years later this school district was given official recognition *for eight years of consecutive improvement*. Leadership's priority was making a positive difference.

Edmonton, with approximately 80,000 students was recognized for its academic *performance relative to expectations*. This district serves an inner-city community with very low socioeconomic indicators; yet, improved student achievement well into the upper half of the province. The superintendent's practice of visiting 7,500 classrooms during four years and discussing teacher improvement programs with school principals was a strategy that greatly benefitted parents in Edmonton.

New York City, another school system working to adopt system accountability for student success, shifted away from the long-standing practice of social promotion. The educational practice of keeping students with their age peers, even when they were academically falling well behind, was a politically correct policy for several decades. McCombs et al. (2010) reported on the city's revised policy for assisting students who were falling behind:

> The policy places considerable emphasis on identifying struggling students early, providing them with additional instructional time, and continuously monitoring their achievement. Students who have been identified as in need of services at the beginning of the school year (based on their performance on the previous year's assessments, teacher recommendations, or being previously retained in grade) are mandated to receive academic intervention services (AIS) in school. In addition, schools can offer a variety of out-of-school support services, including Saturday school (previously called Saturday Preparatory Academies). Students who fail to score Level 2 or higher on the mathematics or ELA assessments administered in the spring are offered several opportunities to meet the promotion standards and can be promoted based on (1) a review of a portfolio of their work in the spring, (2) performance on the summer standardized assessment, (3) a review of a portfolio of their work in August, or (4) an appeal process. Students who do not meet the standards when their portfolios are reviewed in the spring are required to enroll in the Summer Success Academy, which offers additional hours of intensive instruction in mathematics and ELA for several weeks in the summer.

When it came time to report on the results, these authors indicate New York City's success while accepting responsibility for helping their students succeed:

> Scoring at the proficiency level (Level 3 or higher) in NYC schools has increased dramatically, while the percentage of students scoring Level 1 has declined equally dramatically—and this was true across the rest of New York State as well.

Examples:
Mathematics in Grade 7 from 2006 to 2008

- Level 3 (Proficiency): improved by 25 percentage points
- Level 1(well below proficient): declined to 3 percent

English Language Arts in grade 5 from 2006 to 2008
- Proficiency: Improved 17 percentage points

It appears likely that these improvements are related to the set of reforms enacted by the city and state in the NCLB context. *We also found no negative effects of retention on students' sense of school belonging or confidence in mathematics and reading over time.* The near-term benefits we found hold out the possibility of longer term benefits as well.

The RAND Corporation also reviewed New York City policy results and concluded thus:

> Administrators reported that the promotion policy focused the instructional efforts of schools, made parents more concerned about student progress, and provided additional resources to support low-achieving students. Overall, retained students did not report negative socio-emotional effects.

Reviewing this New York study poses an interesting question: How do their students fare in subsequent years? A new report, by the National Center for Education Statistics, compares each state's performance on state tests with their performance on the 2013 NAEP. *New York was the only state that reached NAEP's proficiency range for fourth and eighth graders in both reading and mathematics.* Undoubtedly, this state's results are highly influenced by New York City, and leadership there—that is Mayor Bloomberg—*contributed positive leadership for that education system.*

The point is that *leadership is the critical difference* between school districts making a positive or negative difference in students' education. *Big is not a detriment toward success.* The United States expends a great deal of money into its education system relative to the rest of the world but does not achieve outcomes commensurate with these expenditures. Canada, with its one-third per capita number of school districts but significantly higher levels of student achievement, can provide a model in effective use of funds for administration.

Local control of the American schooling system is a long-standing mantra that is now more connected with political correctness than with reality. The state is now the locus of control with its authority in matters of curriculum and accountability, and the ongoing use of small school districts is actually a waste of taxpayer dollars.

KEY POINTS

- Wasted spending is particularly evident in US school district administration where the number of districts is unreasonably high.
- Local control at the school district level is reduced and replaced by state control.
- High levels of student achievement in several large school districts demonstrate that leadership is the important variable.
- A substantial reduction in the number of school districts across the United States either reduces taxes significantly or provides funding for other programs and services for the government including education.

Chapter 10

Maximizing Students' Work Year

Education is slow to embrace change. Low levels of accountability throughout the school system inhibit the need for change. This book is focused on ways to achieve meaningful change that will overcome political correctness and win educational excellence. Our "global village" environment and perilous economic climate requires rapid response if North Americans are going to experience the *circular cause and consequence* of *learn well, live well*.

Does the amount of time children spend in school matter? Should our governments endeavor to maximize time for learning? Should we continue to pour money into education and pay educators the salaries and benefits currently received? Political correctness is maintaining the status quo rather than taking action. This chapter is about changing an outdated educational practice that is fraught with political consequences from having a pyramidal pinnacle *not inhabited by students*.

The agrarian school calendar, which dominates our education system to this day, *is a perk for educators but a detriment to students.* Today, competition in the global workforce combined with an expanded curriculum requires additional instructional time for all students but especially those from disadvantaged backgrounds. Further, lengthy breaks from instruction hinder the disadvantaged students who then remain disadvantaged in their career choices. The prominent model with its long summer break is not in students' best interests and threatens our potential for *learning well, living well*.

AN OUTDATED SCHOOL CALENDAR

Taxpayers think they own our schools but in too many instances politicians have surrendered practical ownership to teachers' unions during contract negotiations. When collective agreements specify times of day and year when schools are open for students, public control of the school ceases. Enshrining these issues within collective agreements requires expensive trade-offs when attempts to alter these clauses are pursued later. The best interests of students and taxpayers are subjugated to the personal and selfish interests of stakeholders when instructional times are incorporated into contracts.

Few people understand how public perception is cleverly manipulated when unions negotiate teachers' pay and work year. On the one hand, educators compare their compensation to workers in the private sector who have much less job security and, generally, fewer benefits. They also neglect to take into account the number of days they work in a year. Specifically, *how many days in the year are educators required to answer the bell?*

On the other hand, teachers, who enjoy approximately *thirteen weeks* of annual vacation, compare their salaries against workers entitled to only *three or four weeks of* vacation. Such a comparison is further invalidated by the fortuitous timing of teachers' vacations, which coincide with major cultural holidays and the summer weather. Children are not the only ones who enjoy the warm, sunny days of summer. What value should teachers assign to the privilege of having vacations during "prime time," whether these occur during seasons of best weather or periods encompassing major holidays?

When workers compare annual salaries, benefits, such as vacation time, must be factored into the calculation. Generally speaking, teachers' *additional vacation* equates to approximately a 15 percent perk, which is a significant amount of money. There is a myriad of additional benefits in a typical teacher salary package. Pensions, health benefits, paid sick leave, discretionary days, preparation time, as well as many other types of releases from work, both paid and unpaid, can cost taxpayers close to 25 percent of their annual salary.

When private sector workers reference these additional benefits, they are frequently confronted by defensive teachers; however, it is reasonable to consider that all of these benefits, including the lengthy vacation period, provide a perk of approximately 40 percent above the publicized salary. Therefore, an annual *salary* of $80,000 is *valued at* approximately $112,000. Discussions regarding salary comparisons frequently *overlook whether the concept of remuneration involves only money in the pocket or whether benefits are also included.* Any discussion of remuneration that ignores these cost factors is meaningless.

Education's short work year is the focus of this chapter. Unfortunately, our school system continues to organize the school year as though we still live in an agrarian society in which children were required to assist on the family farm. Schools were closed during the summer to facilitate children's work in various farming functions including harvesting crops.

Only a small percentage of our population remains connected to the agrarian enterprise, and almost none of the highly mechanized work involved is performed by children. Moving off the farm and away from agrarian work required our workforce to transition to jobs which required extensive education and a series of skills unknown a century ago.

Surprisingly, while more education is now required to cope in a technologically more complex world, children spend less time in school than they did one hundred years ago because we have adjusted the students' school year to accommodate a variety of professional development activities for teachers. We accept that these activities can be essential for effective teaching but it raises an important question: *Should the school year and vacation schedule be set to deliver teacher benefits or teaching? Should day-long professional development activities be held during teacher or student time?*

Our school system has also *reduced instructional time available for core subjects*. Every societal problem is pushed to our schools for some sort of resolution. Many health-related issues now are addressed within the school day and daily physical education is required to counter the lack of exercise previously addressed by working on the farm. Swimming, family-life education, music, and art are easily recognized programs that are now a common component of a student's workday. In recent years, the social interconnectedness of our lives has added an imperative that children's time in school also addresses their ability to get along with others.

Meanwhile, we have added subjects to the core curriculum in the hope that students will cope with modern life and be better suited to serve national interests. Mathematics and the sciences now dominate many careers, and every learner must be equipped with skills to use technology. All these changes have merit, so drawing attention to them is not intended to denigrate them. Rather, it is to point out that there is a problem.

Learning to live requires so much more than was necessary a century ago. A significant question is whether students are sufficiently prepared during this time when the number of school days is reduced while curricular requirements are increased? In other words, are our children sufficiently prepared to *live well*?

The question is more important now than ever. We need every student to graduate from the school system, and high percentages to proceed to postsecondary learning. Many students are unable to meet graduation standards on time, and they merely meander through the education system falling further behind each year. In a meeting with senior officials of the *US Department of Education*, it was disheartening to learn that the Race to the Top initiative was necessary because in many states the *average student in Grade 12* is leaving with a *Grade 10 level of education*. Those then entering the university system require extensive and expensive remediation.

For example, Education Trust (EdTrust) reports that only 8 percent of US high school graduates in 2009 completed a curriculum that prepares them well for college and the workplace. Even fewer complete those course sequences with grades that would suggest they mastered the content (Gewertz, 2016). Alarmed by the patterns of course taking and grades they saw, the EdTrust researchers concluded that students were "meandering toward graduation with a focus on accumulating credits, rather than on systematically building a strong base of knowledge and skills that will help them thrive after they get their diplomas."

LEARNING AND TIME ON TASK

The 2012 international PISA tests released in December 2013 includes data that reminds us about the importance of students' time on task. Shanghai, China, was the highest performing educational jurisdiction in the world, while the United States was seventeenth in reading, twenty-first in science, and twenty-sixth in mathematics. Notably, Shanghai was *2.5 years ahead* of the highest performing school in Massachusetts, which was the highest performing state in the United States.

Shanghai students attend school for *230 days per year* compared with approximately 180 days in the United States. These international PISA tests are written by fifteen-year-old students who, in the United States, would be in school for their tenth year including kindergarten. During these ten years, Shanghai students received *fifty additional days of instruction per year*. These additional 500 days divided by an American school year of 180 days is equivalent to *2.8 additional years* in the classroom. Canada is only slightly better with a school year of approximately 190 days. To what extent do these additional days in school explain Shanghai's success?

Jensen et al. (2016) researched this issue and prepared their analysis illustrated in figure 10.1. These researchers identified four high-performing jurisdictions—that is, Shanghai, Hong Kong, Singapore, and British Columbia—and demonstrated how many months behind students from the United States, Australia, and European nations were. For example, the performance of the average fifteen-year-old student in America was 22 months *behind* his or her peers in Shanghai and 14 months behind Hong Kong in *reading literacy*. The gap is wider again for science and stretches beyond two years for mathematics.

We expect learning to be positively related with the amount of time children are in school. We have added new and necessary programs, courses, and course content while also increasing the range of student abilities, all of which argue for *more time in school, not less*. The amount of time in school is a student's "resource" and we continually find ways to diminish and trivialize it.

	USA	USA	USA	AUS	AUS	AUS	EU 21	EU 21	EU 21
	RDG	MA	SC	RDG	MA	SC	RDG	MA	SC
Shanghai	22	39	26	18	32	19	22	34	24
Hong Kong	14	23	18	10	17	11	15	19	16
Singapore	14	27	17	9	20	9	14	22	14
British Columbia	11	12	15	7	5	7	12	7	12

Figure 10.1   How many months behind? Differences in PISA performances, 2012

The North American education system seems impervious to the disadvantage perpetrated on children in their global community. We cling to the agrarian calendar because teachers were not required for a full year when our nations were born. Unions have *enshrined this agrarian calendar into their collective agreements*, while winning many additional concessions and driving the costs of education beyond what governments can afford.

School districts serious about reform need to take the true cost into consideration when they identify student achievement as their primary goal. Some US school districts and charter schools are now lengthening the school year for students who are struggling with academic success. *The lengthy vacation period, enshrined in union agreements, is now an impediment to reform because it is considered an entitlement.* As a consequence, the school district has to reduce services, increase taxes, or both in order to maintain necessary levels of learning in a world of accelerating costs.

Politicians must decide the correctness of agreeing with teachers' unions that remuneration be based on comparisons with the private sector whose employees' work many more days per year without the array of benefits, including pensions, enjoyed by teachers. First and foremost, *governments need to acknowledge that their careless management has produced a public workforce whose costs greatly exceed those in the private sector.* Each level of government can recover significant portions of public debt.

In Canada, for example, Leung (2015) reports that the average public sector employee makes 18 to 37 percent more than a comparable employee working in the private sector. This reporting, which compares employee compensation in the private and public sectors found that, when salaries, benefits, and working hours are factored in, a private sector employee costs up to $8,150 less per year, and works up to six hours more each week, compared to someone doing the same job for the government. If government workers were paid at the same rate as their private sector counterparts, Canadian taxpayers would save up to $20 billion a year, according to the report.

This imbalance is even more severe in the United States where CNN Politics on February 19, 2016, conducted a Reality Check during the 2016 presidential debates and reported that wages for similar work were $84,153 for government and $56,350 for the private sector. The checker went on to explain:

> According to the Cato Institute which looks at data from the Bureau of Economic Analysis, the average federal civilian government worker's wages were 49 percent more than the average workers in the private sector in 2014. When comparing total compensation, however, that figure is closer to 78 percent.

These public sector cost factors are used by teachers when negotiating their contracts. Political pandering to education's public sector unions has "dethroned" students from the *pyramidal pinnacle* that describes who our schools are serving. *Learning well, living well* is at risk in North America because other cultures are providing their children with more time to learn. The amount of time a child spends in school is correlated with their success in school so the fewer the days spent in the classroom, the lower the chances of achieving optimal success.

An obvious step is to *reclaim days* within the existing school year when doors are *closed to students* for teachers' professional development, which we have already shown to be relatively meaningless. Achieving this objective does not have to be a cost item but it will challenge leaders inclined toward being politically correct. Negotiations need to focus on the fundamental principle that the *school year is conterminous with the students' work year.*

School days can also be lengthened, if not for all students certainly for those falling behind. Adjusting to longer school days will generate budget issues because teachers will want to be paid for the additional time in the classroom. While not a perfect quid pro quo, teachers' preparation time is another example of how governments have incurred significant costs to further reduce workload for a workforce already advantaged with a short work year. Placing students atop education's pyramidal pinnacle may require some difficult renegotiation to provide some students with additional time for learning.

Finally, lengthening the school year by reducing teachers' thirteen weeks of vacation requires additional consideration. Undoubtedly this extension to the school year will be framed as a budget issue because teachers' unions will argue that thirteen weeks of vacation is an *entitlement in their full-time employment.* Nevertheless, this initiative is truly transformational for education for the purpose of placing North American students on an equal footing with the emerging Asian countries.

The horse is out of the barn on the matter of equating salaries and benefits for teachers and workers in the private sector including the approximate 15 percent differential in work year. Discussion at the political level is required to establish whether teachers can legitimately argue comparisons with full-time workers in the private sector and, at the same time, benefit from thirteen weeks of prime-time vacation. Governments need to initiate the discussion rather than shy away from this contentious issue.

The issue for government is providing students with sufficient time for learning in Canadian and American schools so they remain competitive in a society where learning well and living well is a reality. Extending instructional time will cost money and this book reveals several means for funding this need.

KEY POINTS

- The agrarian school calendar, which dominates our education system to this day, *is a perk for educators but a detriment to students*
- Teachers deem their work year which includes thirteen weeks of vacation to be equal to that of other workers, and they also receive days free from instruction for professional development as well as time during the school day for preparation.
- Shanghai students, who scored the highest results on PISA 2012, attend school for an additional forty to fifty days per year than their North American counterparts.
- Students' time in the classroom should be increased to accommodate additional curriculum and to ameliorate learning deficiencies.

Chapter 11

Unions Belong in the Accountability Tent

The pyramidal pinnacle is referenced on several occasions in this book as a metaphor regarding which group in education sits atop the pyramid. This occupant is discerned by analyzing which group's needs are pursued most vigorously when governments make educational decisions. The group receiving the greatest attention actually qualifies as the school system's client and the overwhelming evidence is that this perch is not occupied by students, parents, taxpayers, or the public, but by teachers and their unions.

Educators are the largest workforce in our society and governments can ill afford to disregard a special interest group with so much political power. *The reality is that teachers can vote and students cannot.* A second reality is that teachers have a natural stage in classrooms to influence students' opinions, which are seldom challenged by politicians or bureaucrats with different perspectives, and *an obligation to shine light* on information, which can challenge a politically correct course.

Teachers' unions exist for the benefit of their members which, on many occasions, have objectives that are inconsistent with their students' best interests. They are controversial in educational politics, and this book's focus includes their success in advancing members' self-interests over students' best interests. The controversy generated is whether they are a *stumbling block to reform* or *advocates for better schools and better teachers.*

Public attitudes regarding this differing perspective are shifting. Peterson et al. (2012) asked Americans the question, "Do you think teacher unions have a generally positive effect on schools, or do you think they have a generally negative effect?" While 41 percent of the public selected the neutral position, those with a positive view of unions dropped to 22 percent in 2012 from 29 percent in 2011. The survey's most striking finding was "that 58 percent of teachers took a positive view of unions in 2011, and only 43 percent do in 2012. *The number of teachers holding negative views of unions nearly doubled to 32 percent from 17 percent."*

These documented declines in union support are from a myriad of issues including several referenced in this book; however, this chapter is focused on three: requirements that workers must belong to a union; public sector organizations' use of strikes to disrupt society; and union leadership's all-consuming focus with securing *more pay for less work* for members: even to the detriment of education's real clients who are parents and their children, first and foremost, and taxpayers who fund the educational enterprise.

CLOSED SHOP

Many teachers in the education system are *required* to give up an aspect of their individual freedom in order to work because of a process frequently described as closed shop: a requirement that employees remain members of the union at all times in order to remain employed. This requirement is *antidemocratic* because teachers are forced into an arrangement from which they cannot escape unless they are willing to leave their employment.

Closed shop can create confusion for the employee. We easily understand how employees are responsible to their employers, but it is puzzling to many employees that *they also work for the union*. For example, employees who refuse to fulfill a union requirement such as picketing can be disciplined, including having their union card canceled, which means they would no longer qualify to work with that employer. Ultimately, closed shop arrangements provide union leadership with a *significant "hammer" over their membership*.

North Americans benefit from their governments' adherence to *principles of freedom*. It seems incongruous that organizations are permitted to limit peoples' freedom to choose. In essence, a closed shop arrangement is similar to the experiences of citizens in countries governed by one political party—for example, China. Allowing people to make their own choices in areas such as government, religion, and *work* should be everyone's democratic right. *Closed shop is the union's ultimate power and control mechanism.*

Across the English-speaking world, notable differences in legislation exist regarding a right-to-teach environment. *At issue is whether teachers have the right to work without a membership component.* Another issue relates to whether a teacher has the right to formally opt out of the union while retaining the right to teach. While there are many issues involved, these two get at the heart of whether countries, states, and provinces operate a closed shop.

In the United States, twenty states have "right-to-work" legislation prohibiting any employer from making union membership a work requirement. The majority of these states are in the southeast quadrant of the country, with additional states located in the Midwest. Other states permit variations of unionization involving issues such as dues, membership in one or more unions, and opting-out provisions. These states tend to be in the northeast industrial regions where trade unionism is strongest.

The commitment to unionism in the United States also reflects differing perceptions teachers have on one of the more contentious issues in the world of education today, namely pay-for-performance based, in part, on standardized test scores. Farkas et al. (2003) report that,

> On virtually every proposal for rewarding teachers differentially, southern teachers are more open compared with teachers in other regions throughout the country. Even when it comes to using standardized test scores to determine teachers' pay—the proposal that was least popular among all teachers—half (50%) of southern teachers favor it, compared with 36% in the Midwest, 34% in the West and just 26% in the Northeast.

In Australia, New Zealand, and Great Britain, union membership is not required, dues are not required, and there are separate organizations dealing with collective bargaining and professional activity. This separation in focus is significant because teachers can pursue their professional development interests without becoming embroiled in issues related to union politics.

The Canadian situation varies from having a province with the most "closed" environment in the English-speaking world to provinces and territories where union membership is optional, dues are not required from nonmembers, and there is only one organization identified to represent teachers choosing to become members. For example, *Alberta legislation* requires that *all public school teachers* be a member of a specific union that conducts activities associated with both negotiations and professionalism. This model demonstrates the most extreme closed shop environment because the government *decrees* that a public school teacher must be a member.

On the other end of the spectrum, Prince Edward Island makes union membership optional (teachers must opt out in writing) and dues are not required from nonmembers. The only opting-in provision is to the one existing organization. This model increases accountability for the union beyond that which is evident in Alberta because teachers can *choose* whether they will join.

Freedom to make decisions is at the heart of this issue because the union's power is enhanced by the closed shop provision. *Absence of choice absents accountability.* Union leadership can push the boundaries of their thirst for power; yet, remain immune from the accountability for improving student outcomes. Their bottom-line mandate of "less work with more pay" for their members does not enhance service to the school system's clients.

Their quenchless thirst for power achieved without concomitant accountability while reducing management's capacity to operate an efficient and effective school system has produced a more toxic environment.

RIGHT TO STRIKE

Striking is the ultimate activity used to persuade management and has been effectively employed in the public sector to curtail management's rights. While unions are successful in their ongoing quest for higher salaries, their push to dictate working conditions (e.g., closed shop, strike, class size limitations, preparation time, work leaves, etc.) is even more successful. Demanding exorbitant salary increases is a cleverly used negotiating tactic followed by trading in some of the salary demands for greater control over *management rights* in the conditions of the workplace.

Union strategy is aimed at having an idea rooted in at least one jurisdiction within a larger region during a cycle of negotiations. In subsequent cycles their battle cry—"If there why not here"—will succeed in bringing many other jurisdictions in line. Sooner or later, all school boards are *whipsawed* into line, and the next issue can be targeted in a similar manner. Over time, not only do financial costs escalate but management's abilities are significantly eroded.

This whipsaw process is greatly facilitated by the teachers' right to strike, which is an important issue in this chapter. Teachers' unions acquired this bargaining tool in the middle of the twentieth century, and many states and provinces now permit teachers to organize and, ultimately, strike. In 1937, US president Franklin D. Roosevelt expressed his opposition to public sector unions having the right to strike when he said:

> The process of collective bargaining, as usually understood, cannot be transplanted into the public service. . . . A strike of public employees manifests nothing less than an intent on their part to obstruct the operations of government until their demands are satisfied. Such action looking toward the paralysis of government by those who have sworn to support it is unthinkable and intolerable.

Was President Roosevelt, a Democrat, merely resistant to change or particularly insightful? It is well known that American unions are aligned with the Democrat Party, and his comments certainly were contrary to that relationship. He understood that the public and private sectors are distinctly different, and the ability to strike provides the former with a significant negotiating advantage over the latter. Serving in a *monopolistic environment* where clients have no other options for accessing services provides public sector unions with powerful leverage.

A shift in political thinking occurred not long afterward. Some states—for example, New York and Wisconsin—had opened the door to public sector unions and, *through the use of a 1962 executive order and not a Congressional vote*, US president Kennedy changed the public sector landscape by introducing organizational representation for federal government workers.

Henninger (2010) refers to the importance of this event because it "swung open the door for the inexorable rise of a unionized public work force in many states and cities. This in turn led to the fantastic growth in membership of the public employee unions . . . and the teachers' National Education Association." In Henninger's opinion,

> They broke the bank. More than that, they entrenched a system of taking money from members' dues and spending it on political campaigns. Over time, this transformed the Democratic Party into a public-sector dependency. *They became different than the party of FDR, Truman, Meany and Reuther.* That party was allied with the fading industrial unions, which in turn were *tethered to a real world of profit and loss.*

President Roosevelt understood how *profit and loss* served as a *check and balance* for dealing with egregious union demands but that this feature is now absent in the public sector. Politicians can pass on to the next generation the implications of their poor management of the public system by piling up annual deficits into long-term debt, increasing taxes, or reducing other programs and services.

Within a few years of President Kennedy's proclamation, Canada opened the door to public sector unions resulting in similar trends. Crowley (2013) expresses his perceptions following a strike by Canadian teachers, and why he believes granting public sector workers a right to strike was a *monumental mistake*:

> Few today even remember that powerful public sector trade unions are a relatively recent creation. And while trade unions before the grant of the right to strike amusingly described public sector labour negotiations as "collective begging," the very special and unusual position of public sector workers makes strikes there unusually damaging to the rest of society.
>
> The problem is with the principle of a right to strike in the public sector, not its use in any particular set of circumstances. So rather than deal awkwardly on a case-by-case basis with the consequences of strikes, *we should get back to fundamentals and ask if they are an appropriate tool for public sector labour relations at all.*

The reason why public sector workers were not entitled to strike before the 1970s was not some fit of forgetfulness where we neglected to include them in a right granted to private sector workers. It was a thoughtful recognition that private sector and public sector employers are simply not the same animal. *Governments exercise a monopoly over the provision of many vital services in a way that virtually no private sector employer ever can.*

If the unionized autoworkers go on strike at GM or Ford or Chrysler, you can still buy a car from (nonunion) Honda or Hyundai or Toyota. If Air Canada goes on strike, you can still fly WestJet or Porter or drive or take the train. But if the nurses, teachers, air traffic controllers or hydro workers strike, the service they represent is withdrawn.

This draws the public into public sector labour disputes in a way that hardly ever occurs in private sector negotiations. *And politicians always have a nervous eye on voters' discontent.* Thus for years public sector workers were essentially not allowed to strike. The consequence of public sector workers effectively wielding a veto over whether public services were available was that the state restricted the damage that power could do.

There is another way in which the public sector employer is different than the private employer. *Companies face the discipline of the bottom line*: they must make money selling goods or services that people want to buy at prices they are willing to pay. If private employers fail this test, they go out of business. Governments cannot go out of business. They pay their bills through taxation, which means *they need not trouble themselves too much about whether people think they are getting good value for their tax dollars.*

Finally, the customers for public services, people using hospitals and schools, for instance, don't pay the full cost of labour settlements the way customers of private sector firms do. The costs of public sector settlements fall on all taxpayers, and those costs are all tangled up in a complex tax burden rather than a straightforward bill for a private service that consumers can understand.

In the *private sector*, union power is in terminal decline as work shifts away from traditional blue collar occupations in natural resources and manufacturing to white collar services where people have more confidence in their own abilities to represent their own on-the-job interests and are more reluctant to see a bureaucratic third party representing their interests to their employers. Free trade and globalization mean that workers and firms in Canada must work together to overcome foreign competition. Their interests are not opposed, but aligned.

The one area of the economy where unionism still holds unchallenged sway is the public sector, and that is because the unique features of government employers and the power that confers on their employees: the politicization of public sector negotiations, the lack of the discipline of the bottom line and the way the cost of labour agreements is spread across all taxpayers.

These differences cry out for a different approach to public sector wage negotiations, *one where strikes have no place.* Governments should not be able to set public sector wages and working conditions unilaterally either, so independent third parties would have to arbitrate the demands of both sides, with the driving force a mirroring of relevant private sector wages rather than the *egregious power of public sector strikes to terrify politicians and harm citizens.*

This profoundly simple and succinct explanation regarding governments' mistake in allowing the public sector, including teachers, the right to strike provides the background for many of the issues within the school system. Educational costs have escalated without sufficient "bang for the buck." Equally significant is the usurpation of management rights by educational employers who are unable to rid the system of incompetence, require people to upgrade their teaching talent, or reward them for their competence.

The right to strike in education has changed teachers and their relationship with the public. *It is the social catastrophe of the last century and the underlying reason why some superintendents say that teachers are now more prone to seeing teaching as a job, rather than their avocation.* There is an aura of trade unionism which is unhealthy. Indeed, some teachers' unions adopted trade union status. By utilizing strikes, there is a level of *strident behavior* witnessed by students, which is unfortunate. There is a loss of service to the public, which is unconscionable.

Politicians brought about this damaging situation because they were willing to trade away society's best interests for their own self-interests. The negative implications of their *pandering for votes* which were controlled by special interests had an impact far beyond the immediate situation. We are now saddled with their lack of insight and selfish behavior. Undoing what was done will be difficult, as is always the case when people take on vested interest groups with political power.

Zwaagstra et al. (2007) articulates this political problem well:

> Teachers' unions do not have fundamental responsibility for the accountability of school systems; rather, that responsibility belongs primarily to those who officially govern school systems. If unions have received too much at the expense of the public, then the fault lies with provincial [state] governments, school boards, parents, and citizens.
>
> Governments are responsible for the legislative and regulatory arrangements that govern school systems, including the powers and duties of school boards and the legal regime for collective bargaining. Every clause in every collective agreement has been agreed to by a school board representing citizens, including parents. If there has been a less-than-effective preservation of management rights, that is something for which school authorities, to a significant extent, are responsible. Parents and citizens, too, bear some significant responsibility for insufficiently accountable school systems when they too easily accept unions' characterizations of what is in the best interests of the public.

Politicians, who gave us this problem, are long gone but their unfortunate legacy remains. Our dilemma is that they are replaced with people who continue to pander passionately to the service providers rather than the clients. "No one can serve two masters" and, if they see their primary commitment is to the provider, they are against the recipient. As harsh as this may sound, it is true. The pandering evident in private sector unions pales in comparison to that in the public, where a *monopoly* over the provision of many vital services is well beyond what a private sector employer could achieve.

Some politicians, frustrated by seeing management lose control of their educational responsibilities, may utter a "mea culpa" while acknowledging their political mistake: a mistake that could have been avoided if they had been more diligent. They might even say that administrators supported unions' demands for more control of management. Zwaagstra et al. (2007) draw attention to this issue:

> School administrators, who are supposed to function as on-site managers, are themselves former teachers and are both more sympathetic to teachers' values and expectations and less attached to their role and responsibilities as managers who must also represent the interests of the employer, parents, and taxpayers.

Confounding these perspectives is a convenient excuse that both politicians and their administrators use when responding to their dilemmas. During teacher strikes, parents exert pressure on politicians and the management to reopen schools regardless of the implications. When parents experience the threat of paying for babysitting arrangements, their usual focus is on persuading those managing the school system to *abandon* their negotiating positions, and do *whatever is necessary* to avoid a strike or end one prematurely. They focus on *today* rather than on "tomorrows."

The problem with these varying perspectives is that they serve as a "smokescreen" to a larger problem. *Management routinely neglects to explain to the public the many issues identified in this book, all of which constrain their effort to provide the most effective education for students.* This neglect is purposeful, however. Making the public aware of these issues usually angers teachers, and understandably so. But by not laying the groundwork for change by helping the public understand the critical, but subtle issues, *politicians and managers undercut their position* with the public and make support for the union inevitable.

It is time to protect the public, parents, and students from the harmful effects of public sector strikes, which leave the public hostage to the selfish desires of a small but vital group in our society. The union's assumption of a monopolistic role in the dispensing of educational services has been abused and the longer our political leaders fail to face financial reality, the worse will be the *long-term damage* this situation will create. Political courage is essential if the unions are to be brought into the system in a way that benefits all, and not just the teachers who are their only mandate.

UNION LEADERSHIP BELONGS IN THE TENT

These notions of removing closed shop and strikes will not be well received by union heads as will not the efforts to increase accountability within the education system. Currently, union officials occupy one side of the "us" and "they" equation leading to contractual agreements, which is a formula producing ongoing conflict. Unions are *preoccupied with inputs* and management should be *focused on student outcomes*, even though the government's innate desire for "peace in the valley" dominates the management's actions.

At a meeting for one province's school superintendents, government representatives explained a political perspective that teachers' support was necessary for winning elections. The message then delivered was that districts give the union what was wanted or government mediators would intervene and indicate where else the disputed provision(s) already existed and, "if there, why not here." Superintendents would be identified as a *stumbling block* to achieving agreement and experience consequences associated with their notoriety. "Peace in the valley" rather than accountability was clearly the politically correct response in this situation.

Accountability in public sector organizations such as education must undergo greater examination. In complex relationships, as are evident in our school system, different types of accountability are involved: some bodies provide funding while others administer it and set policies. When dual accountabilities are evident, the primary accountability is usually to the organization that provides the most funding.

Accordingly, in our North American school systems, three political bodies are accountable in varying degrees. In the United States, the federal government provides a minor portion of the funding whereas, in Canada, funding from the national government is nonexistent. In both of these countries, the state or province is the significant funding source that may be accompanied by taxation powers within the school district. To varying degrees then, politicians are assigned accountability for the quality of services provided in improving student outcomes.

Union leadership does not fit into this accountability paradigm because they do not fund education and there is *no provision for the public to vote them out of office* if there is dissatisfaction with the schools' quality of service. Instead, union leadership is immune to educational accountability and their power and success in limiting the authority of educational managers to improve the system is a significant issue. Without attaching accountability for improving student success to teacher unions, there is a gap in democratic accountability and our education system is at risk.

This description is not a criticism of teacher unions at the theoretic level: they are merely fulfilling their responsibilities and functioning in accordance with their mandate. Their success is well documented. Rather, the concern is focused on what has become an inappropriate relationship where a *lack of accountability is too evident.* Weak and cowardly politicians, who pander for votes by sacrificing excellence in education, *require a new paradigm* because we now live in a global community.

The union's phenomenal success should be a wake-up call for implementing a new accountability structure that *includes union leadership.* In the United States, for example, student achievement is being incorporated into staff evaluations which will be linked with their pay. Linking performance and pay is a revolutionary practice in education, and *a similarly transformational reshaping of union politics is conceivable by aligning union leadership's pay to student outcomes.* Their success at the bargaining table in achieving the status of comanagers of the school system requires that their leadership be held accountable for student success and other outcomes determined and overseen by the public.

Unions are an adversarial special interest group seeking to improve the fortunes of their members; yet, they ardently want to be considered as educational partners. A partnership with the government—which leads and allocates funds—and with parents—who are the system's clients—and the public—who pays the bills—is conceivable. Partners share in the good and the bad. In this partnership, consequences are applied based on the performance recorded on the school system's report card.

Creativity may be necessary to operationalize such a new approach. For example, at the conclusion of the annual reporting cycle, the school district could send the union a financial reward commensurate with the district's report card when various degrees of improved outcomes are achieved. Union management would determine disposition of this incentive award. Various additional options could be explored including negotiated agreements.

There is a second component to this partnership. Political leadership should be removed when system results are not improving and a similar consequence should be applied to the partners providing leadership to teachers. Just as political leadership can be "punted" when the school system fails to deliver quality educational services, so should the partner's leadership be removed.

Legislation should be in place quantifying a failed report card that incorporates principles of progressive discipline beginning with "letters of warning." Additional disciplinary actions should be spelled out; however, eventually key leaders, including union bureaucrats, are removed from their positions.

In this manner, a shared vision replaces the selfishness that currently exists. Trust between the partners increases because accountability for educational excellence is equalized.

Including union leadership in these accountabilities is a novel approach. Unions understand a basic accountability in the private sector where profit-and-loss statements prevail. These statements are lacking in the public sector where politicians merely transfer resources from one department to another or incur deficits and dig deeper into public pockets.

Increasingly, this long-standing approach to *increase spending without return on investment* is becoming politically incorrect and public attitudes are shifting. *Network*, a 1976 American satirical film selected for preservation in the United States National Film Registry by the Library of Congress, is considered "culturally, historically, or aesthetically significant." The film's contribution to society is its famous line, "I'm mad as hell and I'm not going to take it anymore." Union leadership would be wise to approach the education system for a place in the tent rather than wait for political backlash from their constantly selfish pursuits.

KEY POINTS

- Public and teachers' support for unions is declining.
- Closed shop arrangements are antidemocratic.
- The right to strike in a monopolistic enterprise is inappropriate.
- Union leadership's accountability for educational outcomes should be introduced using incentive pay and progressive discipline.

Chapter 12

Accountability for University Departments of Education

The development of the Common Core in the kindergarten–Grade 12 school system was requested by governors in forty-five states and the District of Columbia. This initiative to introduce common standards represents a transformational enterprise with far-reaching effects for American education including reducing grade inflation in our schools. *This problem of teachers having low expectations for their students resulting in unearned high marks is well hidden from students, parents, and the public.*

Inflated grading is perpetuated by a postsecondary system which has an even greater problem, wherein a grade of "A" no longer stands for "excellence" but "average." Normally, recipients of students progressing through the school system would serve as a check and balance for reducing grade inflation but this hypocrisy remains uncontrolled because of the low standards evident in postsecondary education.

A study of 200 colleges and universities found that more than 40 percent of all grades awarded were in the "A" range and that in *Harvard's Education Department the most frequently awarded grade is a straight "A"* (Slavov 2013). Another major study reported on Grade Inflation.com website; grade inflation for American postsecondary institutions are reported for 1992, 1997, 2002, and 2007 demonstrating *incremental increases in grade point average (GPA)* for each five-year segment as follows:

- Public institutions from 2.85 in 1992 to 3.01 in 2007.
- Private institutions from 3.09 in 1992 to 3.30 in 2007.

Validating these findings is another report published on the TakePart website on March 31, 2016: "A's for Everyone: How Grade Inflation Is Wrecking Higher Education" (see figure 12.1).

A report card of straight A's might make parents paying a pretty penny for their child's college education feel a diploma is worth the financial sacrifice. But according to the most comprehensive analysis ever of grade inflation in higher education in the United States, nowadays even the most average students are likely to be given A's. Although all those A's might make American students feel—or appear—smart, in the long run, it could make them less employable compared with their legitimately high-achieving peers around the world.

Indeed, the report reveals that in the 1940s and 1950s, it was normal for students to earn C's, even at Ivy League institutions. But that began to change during the Vietnam era, when professors began giving male students higher grades to keep them from flunking out, which would make them eligible for the draft.

A practice, which may have started to provide a way for avoiding the military draft, now permeates America's postsecondary institutions and this fraud now denies employers a valid screening method of knowing which candidates are the most qualified.

This brief summary of the degree of grade inflation across our universities and colleges is important because reducing standards cheapens the degrees earned; however, the prevalence of this phenomenon within *education's preservice training* institutions is more disturbing. Teachers, who grade students' work in the K–12 school system, come from a *training system rife with inflated grading*.

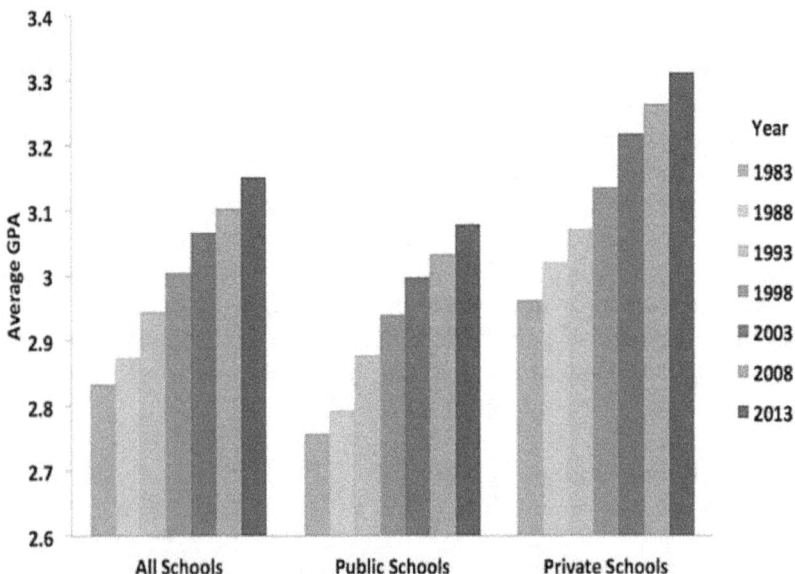

Figure 12.1   Degree of Grade Inflation Across American Colleges and Universities

TEACHERS GRADUATE FROM A SYSTEM PLAGUED BY GRADE INFLATION

Educators may excuse their tendency to inflate grades by pointing out that grade inflation is rampant in their training institutions in universities where marks below "B" seldom occur and failure is virtually nonexistent. Koedel (2011) analyzed major academic departments at universities and reported how education marks are skewed upward (see figure 12.2). *Grade point averages for students enrolled in the department of education were much higher than they were in any other department.*

Koedel found that,

Students who take education classes at universities receive significantly higher grades than students who take classes in every other academic discipline. The higher grades cannot be explained by observable differences in student quality between education majors and other students, nor can they be explained by the fact that education classes are typically smaller than classes in other academic departments. The remaining reasonable explanation is that the *higher grades in education classes are the result of low grading standards.* These low grading standards likely will *negatively affect the accumulation of skills for prospective teachers during university training.* More generally, *they contribute to a larger culture of low standards for educators.* . . . While all other university

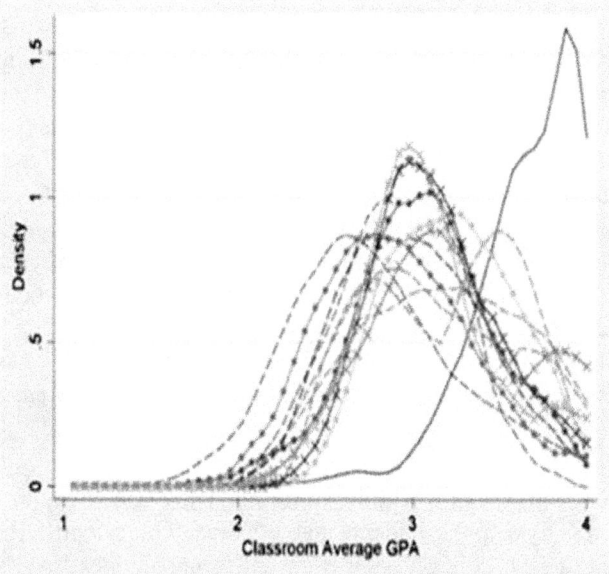

Figure 12.2 Classroom Average Marks in American University Courses

departments work in one space, education departments work in another. . . . The data consistently show that education departments award exceptionally favorable grades to virtually all their students in all their classes.

Babcock (2010) indicates that *grade inflation is associated with reduced student effort* in college: put simply, students in classes where it is easier to get an "A" do not work as hard. He demonstrated that in classes where the expected *grade point average* rises by one point, students *respond by reducing effort*, as measured by study time, by at least 20 percent. The implication for education, therefore, is that *teachers who are being trained know less because their marks are so high.*

Using the data from figure 12.2, Koedel estimates that, "If the grading standards in each education department were moved to align with the average grading standards at their respective universities, student effort would rise by at least 11–14 percent." Koedel provides a hypothesis regarding why education departments having these deplorably skewed results escape detection.

> One notable difference between education departments and other major departments at universities is that virtually all graduates from education departments move into a *single sector of the labor market*--education. If the education sector is less effective at identifying low-quality graduates than are other sectors of the labor market, this would help explain why professors in education departments are able to consistently award As to most students.

Most departments in a university serve a diverse market. For example, the business department seeks to place graduates in an array of firms that can easily discern the differences in the quality of graduates from another institution. *Firms would cease hiring from lower-quality programs forcing instructors to recalibrate their standards.* Education, on the other hand, is a closed system. Graduates are generally employed locally by a school board, which participates in fostering a culture of low standards. Like the university's department of education, the local school district is reticent to distinguish good teachers from mediocre teachers.

Understanding grade inflation is facilitated by assessing why it is now so prevalent. The Minnesota State University Mankato (*Grade Inflation*) website provides a concise analysis of causes evident from research:

1. **Institutional pressure to retain students.** The easiest way to maintain enrollment is to keep the students that are already on campus. The professors, departments, colleges, and even entire universities may implicitly believe that giving their students higher grades will improve retention and the attractiveness of their classes and courses.

2. **Increased attention and sensitivity to personal crisis situations for students.** The most obvious example was the Vietnam War era. Poor grades exposed male students to the military draft. Many professors and institutions adopted liberal grading policies to minimize the likelihood of low grades. Some sources cite this period as the genesis of recent grade inflation as the students of that era are now professors.
3. **Higher grades used to obtain better student evaluations of teaching.** In an increased effort at faculty accountability, many colleges and universities mandate frequent student evaluations of faculty that often end up being published or otherwise disseminated. These same evaluations play an increasingly important role in tenure and promotion decisions. *Faculty members who find themselves in such situations may attempt to "buy" better student evaluations of their teaching by giving higher grades.*
4. **The increased use of subjective or motivational factors in grading.** Factors such as student effort, student persistence, student improvement, and class attendance count in favor of the students who possess these desirable characteristics. *This tends to skew grading patterns upward.*
5. **Changing grading policies and practices.** The increased use of internships, contract grading, individual study courses, group work within courses, a liberal withdrawal policy, generous use of the incomplete grade, and the ability to repeat courses to improve a grade can all contribute to grade inflation.
6. **Faculty attitudes.** A faculty member who believes that grades are a vehicle to please students rather than to recognize and reward performance will tend to give higher grades. Similarly, a professor less willing to distinguish superior work from good or average work will tend to impart an upward bias to grades. One source places most of the blame for grade inflation on the shoulders of faculty who have failed in their traditional role of gatekeepers. The implication here is that it is easier to give a good grade than a bad grade for the instructor.
7. **Content deflation.** For large public universities, the temptation might be to lower both the expectations and the demands in individual courses. A fairly liberal admissions policy, a large number of nontraditional students, and a large number of working students all tempt professors to lower their expectations by reducing the number of textbooks, the amount of writing, and the amount of homework in the course. The goal may be laudable in responding to the particular needs of a specific student body but the result may be inflated grades.
8. **Changing mission.** It is also possible that, as some institutions de-emphasize the teaching mission in favor of the research or service

component, some faculty may be unwilling or unable to spend their time on grading and evaluation. This lack of attention to grading and evaluation could result in a weakening of standards.

These influences on grading student work are negative because *clients of our university and college system are cheated from knowing who are the most qualified* for positions they want filled. Compounding this deception is an equally important issue regarding a reduced work ethic and level of preparedness evident in graduates. An important aspect from this list of potential reasons for the "standards creep" evident in universities and colleges can be summarized from a report provided by Caruth and Caruth (2013):

> It has been suggested that a "grade-leniency theory" exists. That is, *"students buy good grades and faculty buy good evaluations"* in return. Students would appear to be doing less because they do not have to do more to continue getting the higher grades. With college education growing more expensive each year and with students spending less time on their studies, it would seem that the cost of a college education is rising much faster than even realized.

A significant point in this chapter is that the school system is run by people who come through training programs where assessments of their learning are highly inflated. In turn, this culture of low expectations influences how administrators, who are promoted from within teacher ranks, inflate performance evaluations such that almost everyone is rated above average. Finally, this culture of inflated evaluations produces an environment in our nations' classrooms with assessments of students' work also being highly inflated.

PROGRAM MEDIOCRITY

Compounding this environment of low standards is the overwhelming evidence of ineffective programming evident in American preservice programs. The National Council on Teacher Quality provides a comprehensive review of institutions across the United States with damning evidence regarding how poorly prepared many new teachers entering the school system are (Greenberg et al., 2013).

This report concluded that preservice has "become an industry of mediocrity, churning out first-year teachers with classroom management skills and content knowledge inadequate to thrive in classrooms with ever-increasing ethnic and socioeconomic student diversity." It expands on conclusions by stating the following:

- Less than 10 percent of rated programs earn three stars or more (out of four).
- It is far too easy to get into a teacher preparation program. Just over a quarter of programs restrict admissions to students in the top half of their class, compared with the highest performing countries, which limit entry to the top third.
- Just 7 percent of programs ensure that their student teachers will have uniformly strong experiences, by only allowing them to be placed in classrooms taught by teachers who are themselves effective, not just willing volunteers.
- The "reading wars" are far from over. Three out of four elementary teacher preparation programs still are not teaching the methods of reading instruction that could substantially lower the number of children who never become proficient readers, from 30 percent to under 10 percent. Instead, the teacher candidate is all too often told to develop his or her "own unique approach" to teaching reading.
- Fewer than one in nine elementary programs and just over one-third of high school programs are preparing candidates in content at the level necessary to teach the new Common Core State Standards now being implemented in classrooms in forty-five states and the District of Columbia.

This track record *of* low expectations and mediocre preparation in preservice training requires several accountability functions to enhance credibility. Preservice should adopt a similar approach as the school system with *common standards* and then *assessments* of student learning relative to these standards. Employers deserve assurances that graduating teachers from one institution will be comparable with those from others, and students in these preservice programs should be assured that their development will be consistent with professional requirements.

Reforming the culture of low standards requires dramatic action until such time as preservice instructors understand assessment standards. Requiring instructors to adopt a *quota system for student marks* with a minimum of five grading levels is more legitimate than the fraudulent practices currently in place. A quota system for assigning marks is antithetical to a standards approach; however, abolishment of this quota approach occurs when the standards, assessments, and public reporting processes are operational. Fixing a broken system requires dramatic intervention until appropriate checks and balances are in place.

Teacher training programs should also receive constant evaluative feedback from their graduates' employers so that they can adjust the quality of their programs. Prospective students can also use this information to direct their applications for attaining the highest level of training. When accredited graduates are assessed as being "less than satisfactory," in areas of their training, these new teachers should be able to collect on a "warranty" entitling them to *free upgrading from their preservice institution.*

This book is about curtailing political correct activity and achieving educational excellence. Acknowledging that fraudulent assessments permeate the education system is an important step. Being forthright about this disturbing condition is not a virtue within the education system, and politicians are too concerned about losing votes by revealing this flaw to the public. Actions must be taken to improve the accountability of teacher training programs so that our children are better served. Implementing the following policies will produce excellence:

1. Develop a common standards approach for teacher preservice, if not nationally then state or province-wide. A standards approach does not conflict with academic freedom because instructors continue to employ whatever curriculum, resources, or teaching strategies they wish. Standards ensure that trainees have requisite skills and knowledge to be effective practitioners.
2. Implement system-wide standardized assessments for teacher training programs to evaluate trainee learning and publicly report results. Models for these are already prevalent in numerous professions.
3. Require the system of training institutions to develop common policies for assessing preservice teachers using a mark quota system with a minimum of five grading levels.
4. Require school districts to complete a standardized assessment evaluating each new graduate's teaching talent and publicly report results by institution and program—for example, elementary, secondary, fine arts. Principals with recent graduates from preservice should provide training institutions with an evaluation of their "product."
5. First-year teachers receiving "less than satisfactory" evaluations should collect on their "warranty" from their certifying institution with free upgrading.

KEY POINTS

- Universities are plagued by standards creep with especially high levels of grade inflation in their education departments.
- Grade inflation has a negative effect on the university students' work ethic.

- Teachers graduate from institutions with low standards and transfer that culture into their classrooms resulting in high levels of grade inflation for students.
- The teaching profession will benefit from increasing accountability for preservice training.

Chapter 13

Job-for-Life Is a Wrong Practice

"It is true that, when an entitlement begins to be enjoyed by people, they like to keep it."

Jon Kyl's words reflect a problem-facing North American society where too many citizens want some form of payment or security from their government and too many employees expect guarantees from their employers. Entitlement thinking is a curse to excellence, *and public sector employers are the main culprits in spreading the entitlement disease throughout our society.*

Job-for-life is one example where entitlement is straining our public sector and, specifically, education. Tenure was deemed necessary to protect teachers from capricious hiring practices in very small jurisdictions as well as for protection when teaching controversial subject matter. Today, North America is highly inhabited with a mobile worker force where replacing a teacher with an administrator's relative or friend is highly unlikely. Curriculum content, once the purview of individual schools, is now developed for entire states and provinces and poses no threat to teachers' livelihood when teaching government-approved curriculum content.

Every taxpayer should be confident that their dollars are obtaining *the highest quality* of educational services. Every parent cherishes a hope that their child will be instructed by the *best teacher*, not just once in a while but each year. Every school district should be pursuing the best teachers to put in front of their students. Every teacher should feel confident that their employer values their services, *not just in year one after being hired but every year thereafter.*

If there is any perceived ambivalence in committing toward these aspirations, the system is failing in its attempt to be student-centered. It is disingenuous to make lofty claims about intent not supported by action, *but school* districts routinely place less than the best teacher available in front of their students. Even the experienced teacher may no longer demonstrate the same degree of proficiency since being hired. There are no acceptable excuses for failing to provide students with quality education each and every year.

Many generally believe that teaching is the most important profession because it holds our future well-being: *learn well, live well.* Tenure or job-for-life contradicts this belief because it does not hold teachers to the highest standard of performance. One school administrator stated it well when he said, "We also want to keep pushing them, just like we want to keep pushing our kids." Yes, we value education and we expect teachers to push their students toward excellence. *Students should not experience greater accountability than the adults who serve them.* Accountability signals our respect!

Providing teachers with a job-for-life is really unfair to them and contributes to performance evaluations that are grossly inflated and filled with fluff. In the past, teachers were not remunerated for excellent performance so they did not benefit from this type of reinforcement. Now, they work in an environment where everyone is "stroked," because when it comes time to evaluate school administrators, teacher perceptions are a significant measure. Education suffers too much from *mutual backslapping.*

TEACHER EVALUATIONS DEMONSTRATE LOW STANDARDS

Raising this significant issue is not intended to denigrate the teaching profession; it is merely a desire to recognize people in a legitimate fashion for their performance. It is very likely that more evaluations are written on teachers than any other profession. Unfortunately, the evidence is that these evaluations are mainly perfunctory and meaningless. Virtually every teacher passes the test of *minimal competence* in a profession characterized by low standards, and almost all teachers are rated *above average,* which is obviously impossible.

A US study conducted by Public Agenda in 2003 polled 1,345 schoolteachers on a variety of educational issues, including the role that tenure played in their schools. When asked, "Does tenure mean that a teacher has worked hard and proved themselves to be very good at what they do?" a response by 58 percent of the teachers polled answered no, tenure "does not necessarily" mean that. In a related question, 78 percent said a few (or more) teachers in their schools "fail to do a good job and are simply going through the motions." *Teachers understand that tenure is not equated with excellence.* In fact, it is not even indicative of satisfactory performance.

The McGrath Training Systems website summarizes why they perceive tenure to be an "awful" characteristic in the education system:

For more than 20 years, we have been gathering the responses of 150,000-plus school site administrators to our anecdotal survey regarding the performance of school district teachers, and their evaluations. *We have found that between three percent and five percent of permanent teachers are functioning in the lowest category of "poor." Another thirteen percent to twenty percent need improvement to meet satisfactory performance and can be considered marginal.* However, school site administrators admit that in their districts, the number of teachers who receive an unsatisfactory performance rating can be counted on one hand, *with several fingers spared*. So, an average of twenty-five percent of teachers nationwide has some need for performance improvement, but do not receive an evaluation that reflects that. Therefore, no improvement occurs. *That is the scandal.*

McGrath's research demonstrates that having a tenured teacher in front of a class is no guarantee that students will receive quality instructional services. However, tenure is a bedrock issue with unions. While holding tenaciously to this practice absolutely refutes that they are student-centered, they know that they hold the upper hand in protecting their members. *Excellence is not their mantra; protection is.* Their ability to control management is a higher priority than the well-being of the nation. They want the public to believe that teaching is the most important profession but their actions demonstrate a different perspective.

Some educators undoubtedly chafe at the suggestion that teachers, in most instances, receive a job-for-life. Occasionally these objections are legitimate; however, new teachers in most regions receive a permanent contract that is for life unless layoffs are necessary. These staff reductions are the result of extenuating circumstances that happen occasionally and cannot be avoided. The irony is that the longer a teacher is employed and possesses many years of seniority, the more unlikely he or she will experience even the threat of a layoff.

Proponents of tenure argue that tenure protects teachers from being replaced by less expensive and, presumably, less skilled new teachers. *This argument is indicative of the fallacy surrounding the myth that experience is the determinant of excellence.* If such was the case, why would employers want to replace an older *superstar* with a younger, inferior teacher? The answer is simple! Until recently, education did not formally recognize that some teachers are superior to others, and we did not utilize measures of superior performance in holding educators accountable, or *even in celebrating their talent*.

Debating tenure necessitates responding to a central question not particularly understood in public debate. *Are teachers interchangeable?* Putting aside differences in specialization such as having a social studies teacher teach mathematics, are accredited teachers equally competent? Parents understand that there are differences in teacher competence but is this awareness fully understood? Hanushek et al. (2005) quantify teachers' impact on student achievement:

Good teachers increase student achievement. The average student who has a good teacher at the 85th quality percentile can expect annual achievement gains that are 0.22 standard deviations greater than the average student with a median teacher. Good teachers do well with students at all levels of achievement, *and there is no evidence that teacher education contributes to quality teaching.*

This conclusion compares teachers viewed as good against those viewed as medium. What about those below medium and how much impact on student success occurs when there is such variance in performance? Hanushek's conclusion is that "the estimated difference in annual achievement growth between having a good and having a bad teacher can be *more than one grade-level equivalent in test performance.*" This large discrepancy in student success should be a concern for any parent but can be even more alarming when the experience is repeated.

Too frequently the "dance of the lemons," which describes how *poor teachers* are frequently moved from one school to another, places them in schools serving low socioeconomic students. Their parents appear to be less likely to complain about the quality of their child's teacher. One superintendent observed how, when his district went through the annual year-end transfer of teachers, problem teachers tended to be placed in the district's poorer areas.

Dillon (2011) reported on Michelle Rhee's reform efforts in teacher evaluation in the District of Columbia noting that 35 percent of the teachers in the city's wealthiest area were rated "highly effective" compared with only 5 percent in the poorest. The chances are disturbingly high that students in the lower socioeconomic regions will experience several years with mediocre teachers. In effect, a risk for these students living in these poorer areas is that increased exposure to mediocrity exacerbates their likelihood of lower levels of achievement and increased likelihood of remaining poor.

The mistake made by the public is their belief that "as long as there is an accredited teacher—any teacher—in front of the classroom, students are being served adequately" (Weisberg et al., 2009). The assumption that teachers are interchangeable is reprehensible because,

> School systems wrongly conflate educational access with educational quality; the only teacher quality that schools need to achieve is to fill all of their positions.... Give high need students three highly effective teachers in a row and they may outperform students taught by three ineffective teachers in a row by as much as 50 percentile points.

In Washington, DC, Nuckols posted at *Huffington Post* on September 21, 2012, that School Chancellor Rhee's reform for dealing with underperforming teachers culminated in the dismissal of almost 1,000 teachers during her three-year tenure. Between the years 2007 and 2013, *The Washington Post* released student achievement test results for DC showing scores of *Proficient* or *Advanced* improving from 27 percent to 50 percent in mathematics and from 34 percent to 47 percent in reading. Dismissing more than one-quarter of the district's teachers produced phenomenally improved levels of student achievement.

Jensen and Reichl (2011) provide additional perspectives regarding teachers' potential for making significant contributions to student achievement:

> Conservative estimates suggest that a student with a teacher at the 75th percentile of effectiveness (measured with a value-added metric) will achieve in three-quarters of a year what a student with a teacher at the 25th percentile will achieve in a full year. A student with an excellent teacher (at the 90th percentile) would achieve in *half a year* what a student with a less effective teacher (at the 10th percentile) will learn in *a full year*.

Barber and Mourshed (2007) summarize the vast differences they discovered when comparing student success during instruction from high- and low-performing teachers:

- High-performing teachers have students progress three times as fast as when with low-performing teachers.
- In primary grades, students placed with consecutive low-performing teachers suffer educational loss that is *irreversible*.
- A teacher's level of literacy, as measured by standardized tests, affects student achievement more than any other measurable teacher attribute.

It is safe to say that these gains or losses, as the case may be, are cumulative when students benefit or are disadvantaged with a preponderance of higher- or lower-level performing teachers.

This discussion about the vast differences in success experienced within teacher ranks is really about *employers abrogating their socially mandated right and responsibility to manage the resources in our educational systems in a way that benefits children.* There are many occasions during contract negotiations when the employer demonstrates whether or not the outcome will be *student- or employee-centered*. Providing teachers with a job-for-life is an example of an irresponsible giveaway that neither serves the client nor reflects good management.

Schools perpetually look for improvement strategies which, unfortunately, usually increase expenditures in frivolous and unjustified ways, just as politicians are prone to do in other spheres of public finance. Rather than tackle reforms that will improve quality and achieve better services at a lower cost, administrators shy away from tackling *entrenched* and sensitive systemic issues, such as tenure, preferring instead to appeal to opportunistic politicians to provide increased funding. Whenever they do this, they contribute to the rapidly rising cost of education and *create benefit for special interest groups rather than students.*

THE SUCCESS OF TEACHER UNIONS

Teacher unions are complicit in this matter because they are more focused on their mandate to protect their members, especially the weaker ones, than they are on providing students with quality education. It is not an exaggeration to say that unions have been extremely successful in providing their members with a job-for-life.

Using a *whipsaw strategy* that played one employer off against others and then claiming, "if there, why not here," unions gradually handicapped the educational system. For this reason, and others outlined in this book, it is not possible to believe their claims of having the students' best interests in mind and their protestations that they know best what is needed to improve the system.

Unions represent a powerful political force that takes advantage of an *uninformed* public who do not understand the stark difference in objectives between the well-intentioned teacher in their school and the quenchless thirst for power exhibited by union leaders. Their position of power is enhanced when their thirst is accompanied by the *right to strike*, which inconveniences parents who require custodial care for their children.

When parents and their children are *held hostage by a withdrawal of educational services*, they have little understanding of the complex issues the employer is attempting to ameliorate. Their impatience is frequently verbalized by comments such as, "Just get this settled!" Parents' desperate need for children's custodial care during a strike is the union's trump card in achieving their outcomes.

Providing teachers with a job-for-life suggests that teachers are essentially infallible. The implication is that their *intrinsic motivation to excel is high every day, every month, and every year for several decades.* In addition to this, it holds that the teacher will immediately pursue improvement in the workplace as education changes. It also assumes that curriculum changes will be implemented vigorously even when a teacher is within five years of retirement. In reality, however, their personal perspectives and circumstances, which made them such desirable employees at hiring, may not remain so for decades without additional pressure being applied to their motivation.

Above all, the job-for-life situation in education is a condition that says all other professions have it wrong. At least, careers outside of the public sector have it wrong, because the private sector has accountabilities that provide a check and balance throughout a career. If clients do not value someone's services, they will not engage in a contract to employ that company or individual, whether it is to fix their car, toilet, eyes, or build their house.

People working in sales understand how quickly accountability impacts their work. Many work in jobs where commissions are the only income: if nothing is sold nothing is earned. There also are examples within the sales sector of companies releasing the bottom producer at the end of each month. The virtual job-for-life environment in education is in stark contrast to the accountabilities in the private sector and is a working condition of incalculable worth; yet, it was once identified as the reason for lower salaries in the public sector.

The adequacy of a job-for-life approach within education could be tested by principals if they put a sign-up list on the school door for their child's next year's teachers. Variances in the number of clients signing up for teachers would make the principal's task unbearable. The most latitude available to parents in this regard is for the principal to let parents know that a request can be initiated, but with no guarantee that it will be accommodated.

From experience, many parents are leery about the ramifications of attempting to avoid specific teachers and will not initiate a request, and the principal is able to accommodate requests from those who have. Unfettered choice accommodated by posting sign-up sheets would create administrative havoc such as principals forcing students into specific classrooms.

Job tenure for teachers has destabilized the working relationship with the employer and shifted the balance of power to the employed. A superintendent explained the consequences of this imbalance when he repeated his trustees' instructions. They saw every hiring decision as a thirty-five-year commitment. Therefore, he was literally ordered to meet personally with every potential new hire before contracts were signed so that he would become accountable for the selection. Whenever a problem occurred with a teacher, board members immediately queried whether this superintendent had vetted the selection personally.

In order to protect himself, this superintendent began to contact various agencies and organizations in an effort to discover the most powerful "listen-for" in the candidate's responses. Recruiters were trained in this technique, and went through the same process hundreds of times annually to ferret out teachers who could verbalize how they implemented desirable teaching characteristics.

Whatever methods school districts use to identify talented teachers, there are no guarantees that the new hires will possess the same talent a few years later. A principal demonstrated a systemic weakness in education when he responded to a question of why his school was selected as the top school in America. It was not an advantaged school serving a high socioeconomic community. Rather it was situated along the US/Mexico border in San Diego with a diversified student population. Walking through the school and interacting with students revealed how special this school was and why news media networks were descending upon this community.

The principal's response to why the school was so successful was worthy of the secrecy he used in providing it. Rather than blurt out a comment for all those assembled, he convened a one-on-one meeting in the privacy of his office where he had a better chance of controlling the consequences of verbalizing his confidential response. The bottom line, in his opinion, was that every teacher on staff was working on *a one-year contract*. Theirs was not a job-for-life! Indeed, if the contract was not renewed, they were released from the school district as well.

This charter school produced performance at a high standard resulting in public adulation. Children *were* the first priority. This gave his school an unfair advantage because other schools were unable to achieve similar high levels of service. Was being fair to their students unfair and wrong? Should this community be penalized by having their school downgraded to the level of schooling provided across the region or the nation? Should other schools not benefitting from this provision receive an apology from the school district's administration for not being able to provide a similar service to their children?

The answer to these questions is obvious. When we know a best practice, it should be made available to every learning environment. It is justified to borrow the union's battle cry: "If there, why not here?" Politicians should have the courage to respond accordingly, but they hesitate because it will cost them votes in their next election and funding for their campaigns. Most compromise their principles by choosing the politically correct path and favoring special interests and not their students.

Whatever the well-meaning intentions were initially, today the main function of tenure is to subjugate students' rights and help poor teachers keep their jobs. Former DC school chancellor Michelle Rhee (2008) bluntly portrayed tenure as "the holy grail of teacher unions, but it has no educational value for kids; it only benefits adults."

Once a teacher is assured of tenure his or her motivation to excel is lost. Teachers today not only decide how and when there will be a change in practice or in the implementation of the curriculum, but they also decide whether such change will even take place. Providing high levels of service to students is less likely because employment uncertainties are almost nonexistent. As long as the teacher is assessed as being *minimally* competent, he or she survives.

It may be that for many the idea that teachers in the public system would work under the same conditions as those employed in charter schools is too radical. This would mean contracts could be for as short a period as ten months. However, *it does not seem unreasonable to ask that contracts be set at three to five years, and not for life.* Teachers who continue to practice their craft proficiently could qualify for contract renewals within their *district knowing that they are perceived as valuable when a new contract is issued.* A sense of fulfillment is more likely to occur when there are more frequent opportunities to express appreciation for a level of service.

Another approach is to establish a teacher evaluation system that *employs multiple ratings.* Many systems only utilize a pass or fail conclusion. In a multiple rating system, teachers with the higher ratings might qualify for a two- or three-year contract for "satisfactory" performance but receive accreditation involving a longer term—for example, five years—for "outstanding" performance. This type of system acknowledges that no one is immune from societal factors that result in lower levels of performance in their work.

THE TENURE TIDE IS CHANGING

Proponents of tenure may argue that employers have ample opportunity to assess teaching talent while the teacher is on probation: usually the first one or two years of their employment. But is it realistic to assume strong performance will follow for more than three decades? Garrett (2008) reporting on a University of Washington study related to reinventing public education found "that the first two to three years of teaching do not predict post-tenure performance." Our workplace in a global village is complex and it is not surprising that our workforce must be flexible in meeting changing needs.

Motivation to change practices frequently emerges from data demonstrating intolerable situations. Weisberg et al. (2009) with the New Teacher Project found that 81 percent of school administrators knew a poorly performing tenured teacher at their school. This study indicated that the untenable revelation is the result of 86 percent of administrators indicating that they did not pursue dismissal of teachers because of the costly and time-consuming process. McGuinn (2010), for example, reported that it can take up to 335 days to remove a tenured teacher before the courts get involved.

A few American politicians are now *rattling this cage* and attempting to remove tenure. On July 24, 2009, US president Barack Obama and secretary of education Arne Duncan announced the Race to the Top program. This initiative made available $4.35 billion in grants to "encourage and reward States that are creating the conditions for education innovation and reform."

Requirements for states to receive funding from the new federal program included adopting policies that take into account student achievement when evaluating teachers, and having plans to remove "ineffective tenured and untenured teachers."

This pronouncement precipitated attitudinal shifts in places such as New York City, where Baker (2012) summarized the changing landscape in the *New York Times:*

> Nearly half of New York City teachers reaching the end of their probations were denied tenure this year, the Education Department said on Friday, marking the culmination of years of efforts toward Mayor Michael R. Bloomberg's goal to end "tenure as we know it." Only 55 percent of eligible teachers, having worked for at least three years, earned tenure in 2012, compared with 97 percent in 2007. An additional 42 percent this year were kept on probation for another year, and 3 percent were denied tenure and fired. Of those whose probations were extended last year, fewer than half won tenure this year, a third was given yet another year to prove themselves, and 16 percent were denied tenure or resigned.

An apple is frequently used as a symbol for education, and an idiom describing this trend away from tenure is that a *bite into the apple has revealed a worm.* In other words, something viewed from the outside, as a good thing, has turned out to be bad. More lawmakers are demonstrating courage to tighten the requirements for earning and keeping tenure. Idaho removed tenure entirely, and Florida requires all newly hired teachers to earn an *annual* contract. New Jersey also overhauled its tenure laws making it easier to fire teachers for poor performance.

These states will be watched by others who may then determine whether they, too, will gain more support than is lost. This is the nature of politics that cannot be underestimated. It is impractical, and perhaps too counterintuitive, to think that politicians will respond automatically in doing something that is in the best interests of students merely because it is in the longer term best interests of the state or nation. Political decisions, it seems, have to be put onto the balance scale to determine where the assets are greatest.

Perhaps politicians will receive sufficient motivation to discontinue the practice of providing tenure when the conclusions of the Howell et al. (2011) survey of 2,600 Americans are widely circulated; it revealed from the opinionated responses that 49 percent opposed teacher tenure while 20 percent supported it. Despite this weak public support for tenure, the reality that politicians face is that tenure is the *Holy Grail* for teachers which, by itself, can determine where a teacher will place an "X" when they are in the voting booth. Everyone supports accountability until it is in their own place of work.

On the other hand, few members of the general public are similarly focused on this issue when they decide where the "X" should go. A politician's election promise to remove teacher tenure may not be their determining factor in where to place the "X" on the ballot. On the other hand, teachers comprise a large work group within the workforce and politicians have to weigh the consequences of alienating them on an issue that will galvanize their opposition.

If the political route is too difficult, there may be a glimmer of hope on another horizon if what Knowles (2010) writes is generalizable across school districts regarding a survey of teachers in the American Federation of Teachers.

> The good news is that the majority of teachers are not interested in protecting colleagues who don't belong in the classroom. Last summer the American Federation of Teachers surveyed its members, asking: "Which of these should be the higher priority: working for professional teaching standards and good teaching, or defending the job rights of teachers who face disciplinary action?" According to Randi Weingarten, the union's president, "by a ratio of 4 to 1 (69% to 16%), AFT members chose working for professional standards and good teaching as the higher priority." She elaborated: "Teachers have zero tolerance for people who . . . demonstrate they are unfit for our profession."

Knowles indicates that in the United States, between 0.1 percent and 1 percent of tenured teachers are dismissed annually, according to the Center for American Progress. His conclusion is that,

> The time has come to eliminate tenure. We are facing monumental challenges in our quest to provide all students with an education that will prepare them to compete in a globalized economy. By removing one of the main sources of friction between labor and management, we can focus on the substantive issues: training, evaluating and rewarding teachers to make teaching a true profession.

According to Knowles, tenure is "one of the main sources of friction between labor and management."

The bottom line in this debate about tenure for teachers is that good practitioners will always be sought by employers. *It is the weak ones who are protected by tenure provisions.* Is this the right focus? Is this practice providing the best service to our nation's children? The union's *Holy Grail* is finally being challenged, and momentum to serve students' interests more than staff's self-interests will increase.

Having a formal celebration event occur routinely every few years, where the employer's representatives confirm that they want the employment relationship to continue, is a more meaningful affirmation of someone's contribution. An employer's commitment to renew the relationship is the highest form of praise next to those relationships based entirely on commission, where value is communicated almost instantaneously.

KEY POINTS

- Teachers enjoy a job-for-life benefit once they acquire permanent status and, once in receipt of a permanent contract, a teacher needs only to perform at a minimum level of competency.
- There are substantial differences in student achievement when with low- or high-performing teachers.
- Giving teachers a job-for-life is a tragic example of how management has lost control of the educational system.
- Providing teachers with a job-for-life suggests that teachers are above human fallibility.
- This benefit requires employers to make a significant hiring decision realizing that it could be for three decades.
- Conditions leading to a perceived need for tenure are rarely applicable to teachers in the K–12 school system.
- The main function of tenure has been to subjugate students' rights and help poor teachers keep their jobs.
- Removing tenure from contracts will cost taxpayers a substantial amount of money.
- Some governments are removing tenure provisions in order to better meet the needs of their students.
- Many teachers acknowledge that tenure is protecting poor teachers, and indicate support for a change.
- America's Race to the Top program is changing current practice regarding tenure.

Chapter 14

Rewarding Performance

Many teachers leave the teaching profession prematurely because they are not rewarded appropriately in the current system that pays teachers according to *inputs* of *experience* and *credential*. Paying teachers on the basis of *achieving improved student outcomes* is gradually working its way into education and progress toward this goal must be maintained or even accelerated. Implementing this approach is more likely to occur when administrators, *school trustees, and politicians are also rewarded on the basis of school outcomes*.

This effort to change the way teachers are paid is controversial because the current basis is *without any accountability* and replacing it with something where accountability exists creates anxiety. Many teachers are accustomed to receiving many years of annual additional remuneration by *getting older on the job* as well as *increasing their credentials* through additional years at the university. The assumptions are that these two criteria are predictive of higher levels in teacher proficiency, but are these beliefs accurate?

TEACHERS' PAY

Teacher salaries are complicated by the philosophical assumptions embedded in union agreements. One of the most pernicious is that *all participants in the grid should receive the same compensation*, which means that teachers working in a region with the same level of education and years of experience receive the same salaries. Presumably, everyone at that level on the grid is equally competent and effective, which we know is absolutely false. They are not interchangeable!

While the situation is gradually changing in the United States, this grid approach prevents employers from *recognizing, rewarding, or incentivizing talent.* Compensation should recognize contribution, and the educational system is prevented from celebrating teacher worth in enhancing their students' success.

Jensen and Reichl (2011) studied the value of current processes designed to recognize teacher success, and conclude that current approaches in appraisal and feedback are ineffective:

> Teachers' appraisal doesn't improve teaching: over 60% of teachers report that appraisal of their work has little impact on the way they teach in the classroom. . . . Teacher appraisal is just an administrative exercise with no feedback to improve student performance: over 60% of teachers report that appraisal of their work is largely done simply to fulfill administrative requirements. . . . Effective teaching is not recognized: over 90% of teachers report that the most effective teachers in their school do not receive the greatest recognition, and *that if they improved the quality of their teaching they would not receive any recognition.*

These authors remind us that our current system of appraising teachers is not only ineffective and that superior teachers are not rewarded, *but that improving teachers would not receive appropriate recognition.* Union agreements that treat everyone the same are counterintuitive to how people should be recognized and rewarded.

In the case of most teachers there is a base pay earned by qualifying to teach, and then there are supplements teachers receive as they acquire additional university degrees and experience. In fact, we can generalize that teachers receive a *bonus* for acquiring additional certification and getting older on the job. These two criteria are the basis for pay differentiation and reward. Until recently, job performance was irrelevant and, where some states are incorporating student academic success as part of teacher evaluations, controversy exists regarding the political correctness of now differentiating salary based on outcomes.

This current debate on teachers' pay is gaining prominence because of the use of standardized testing across North America. Previous attempts to implement merit pay schemes largely failed because assessments of teacher performance were subjective and based on the school principal's evaluation of a teacher. Too many differences in opinion regarding a teacher's competence were evident, and there was too little agreement on which competencies mattered. *Subjectivity encourages bias, which leads to unfairness, and many teachers questioned their principal's judgment when determining teacher merit.*

Rather than recognize classroom performance and student success, in particular, merit pay programs focused on a teacher's contribution outside of their classroom. For example, teachers might earn favor with their principal if they assumed additional responsibilities such as coaching or leading professional development activities. These duties are helpful in the school, but *success in teaching students should always be the final arbiter in determining worth, and therefore salary.*

When school districts first introduced merit-based pay scales, which focused on individual activity rather than group success, there was limited benefit. A sense of team was lost and a competitive teacher environment developed. There were winners and losers, and teachers recognized that if they helped a colleague it might be to their own detriment. Team orientation, which is so necessary in a school environment, where teaching staff are encouraged to learn from each other, was replaced by distrust and rivalry.

The necessary preconditions for merit pay were not yet in the system. Without standardized forms of measurement involving each grade, evaluations focused on *raw* scores rather than *gains*. The former is confounded by the students' socioeconomic status, which is beyond the school's control. The latter is what matters. The critical question—and the one that should impact pay—is whether or not *students have experienced a gain, and this is within the power of a school to produce.*

From a political perspective, implementing merit pay was important but for the wrong reason. At a time when there were calls for increased accountability in education, school systems pointed to merit pay schemes as a step in that direction. Politicians secured community support by demonstrating a commitment to greater accountability, which could also lever additional funding from governments to satisfy special interest groups. There was justification to spend more, ostensibly, because there was greater accountability in schools and demonstrated improvement is a lever for increasing levels of funding.

CURRENT PAY BONUSES ARE WRONGHEADED

Having outlined the need to use empirical data in evaluating a teacher and then the need to take results into consideration when determining an appropriate salary for the teacher, it remains necessary to debunk the pernicious idea that still plagues the system: paying teachers for getting older and acquiring more education. Changing from inputs to outcomes represents a major philosophical shift, and political parties cannot avoid attempting to capitalize on the controversy.

These two aspects have been in use for decades and have cost taxpayers large sums of money, but without justification. Indeed, the focus contributed to less than excellent service for our children because teachers are rewarded for things that do not yield results. Educators differentiate their students' success but many resist attempts to differentiate their success in helping students succeed.

Educators are like other humans and respond positively to extrinsic motivation such as pay. Actually, *extrinsic motivation* in the form of money is already evident in the current payment program for teachers where they are incented to pursue additional degrees. Our studies found that more teachers pursued additional degrees in regions where these garnered greater increases in salary. Additional remuneration is a sufficient incentive or bonus for many teachers to acquire a master's degree.

Hughes-Jones et al. (2006) also examined the issue of certification across three US states and concluded that "teachers' graduate degrees had no significant effect on student achievement." Buddin and Zamarro (2009) reviewed several criteria used for determining teacher pay and concluded the following:

> Teacher effectiveness is typically measured by traditional teacher qualification standards, such as experience, education, and scores on licensure examinations. RAND researchers found no evidence that these standards have a substantial effect on student achievement in Los Angeles public elementary, middle, and high schools. Alternative measures of teacher qualifications and different kinds of reward systems might be more effective at improving teacher quality. *Traditional teacher qualifications have little influence on classroom achievement.* . . . When the researchers analyzed student achievement data along with teacher qualifications, they found that a five-year increase in teaching experience affected student achievement very little—less than 1 percentage point. Similarly, the level of education held by a teacher proved to have no effect on student achievement in the classroom.

Harris and Sass (2008) conducted their analysis of experience and certification indicating that increased certification may even have a *negative effect* on student achievement.

> Like other recent work, we find generally positive, but mixed, evidence on the effects of experience and little or no evidence of the efficacy of advanced degrees for teachers. We find that the first few years of experience substantially increase the productivity of elementary and middle school teachers but have little impact on the effectiveness of teachers at the high school level. Only in the case of *middle school math* do we find that obtaining an advanced degree enhances the ability of a teacher to promote student achievement. For all other grade/subject combinations the correlation between advanced degrees and student achievement is negative or insignificant.

Greene (2005) examined the certification issue labeling it a *myth*, and summarized his review regarding the importance of experience on teaching effectiveness:

Abell Foundation found that teachers holding master's degrees did not produce higher student performance (except for high school teachers with master's degrees in the subjects they taught, as opposed to degrees in education). The evidence seems to indicate that teachers get a little more effective in their first few years as they get up to speed in the classroom, but that after this initial period teachers do not tend to get more effective with more years of experience.

Goe and Stickler (2008) similarly assessed the value of teachers pursuing additional certification and concluded:

The effects associated with a teacher's possession of an advanced degree are *strikingly counterintuitive,* especially given the salary incentives offered to encourage teachers to pursue graduate degrees. Not only do recent empirical studies not find a substantial benefit for students of teachers with advanced degrees, but the majority of such studies also indicate that teachers with master's degrees and beyond may negatively influence their student's achievement.

Roza and Miller (2009) differentiated the value of pursuing additional certification between subject areas and reported:

On average, master's degrees in education bear no relation to student achievement. Master's degrees in math and science have been linked to improved student achievement in those subjects, but 90 percent of teachers' master's degrees are in education programs—a notoriously unfocused and process-dominated course of study. Because of the financial rewards associated with getting this degree, the education master's experienced the highest growth rate of all master's degrees between 1997 and 2007.

Divestment should be part of an effort to distribute compensation differently, in ways that offer greater benefit to students. Teachers currently finance their master's degree studies in anticipation of *guaranteed* financial returns, but if teachers anticipated higher pay based instead on enhanced ability to boost student achievement, their interests would be better aligned with those of their students.

In the fiscal climate ahead, school systems serious about improving results for students will have no choice but to reconsider their long-automated ways of spending money, uncover how much money is at stake, and compare current ways of spending to alternative ones with greater potential to benefit to students.

We could go on at great length about these two issues and the rewards they bring. What is noteworthy is the *absence of research that justifies the use of increased experience beyond the first couple of years and the acquisition of additional degrees as a reward for excellent service.* Michael Bamesberger reported in the *Nebraskan* (2011) the conclusions of the *US secretary of education* as well as those of an American philanthropist:

In November (2010), U.S. Education Secretary Arne Duncan singled out the $8 billion spent on master's degree bonuses annually as *wasteful*, claiming there is "little evidence teachers with master's degrees improve students' achievement more than other teachers—with the possible exception of teachers who earn masters in math and science," according to a speech he gave to the American Enterprise Institute. Microsoft founder Bill Gates also came out in opposition to the bonuses, citing a University of Washington study in which master's degrees in education were found to bear no relation to student achievement.

While the issue of pay receives considerable attention in the United States, only a few Canadian studies are available. In 1997–1999, Canada tested students in reading, mathematics, and science, and collected survey results from students and teachers. Using the teacher data and measuring the performance of students scoring at level three—the passing score—or better, Alberta's students scored the highest and had the greatest percentage of teachers with *less* than five years of postsecondary education. Coincidentally, Alberta's teachers had the country's *lowest pay differential between a bachelor's and a second degree.* By implication, therefore, teachers in Alberta were *less motivated* by degrees and experience than were teachers in other jurisdictions.

A few years later in 2007, the Council of Ministers' Education Canada undertook another review of student achievement in reading relative to teacher education levels. In this instance, students with teachers possessing a BEd degree and some additional nonformal training scored significantly higher than did students in classes where the teacher possessed a graduate degree. *One explanation for this counterintuitive result is that teachers with advanced degrees may become more interested in advancing their careers through administration rather than advancing skills for the classroom.* Coursework then may be a distraction to their efforts in acquiring classroom expertise.

This study also included an examination of student achievement relative to the teachers' years of experience. Teachers were categorized into five-year increments of experience with "twenty or more" representing the highest category. Statistical analysis revealed that there was no correlation between increased student achievement and teacher experience, except in the most senior category, namely "twenty or more years." The other groups scored at the same level, which demonstrates that *only after many years of experience is there a correlation with higher student achievement.*

In 2010, there was another review of student achievement compared with years of teaching experience within Alberta. Some of these teachers were hired to the province from other provinces, but their familiarity with the provincial curriculum and standards for thirteen-year-old students was lacking. During the years 2005–2010, the percentage of teachers *with less than five years of experience* increased each year rising from 26 percent to 41 percent, and decreased annually for teachers with more than twenty years of experience dropping from 29 percent to 21 percent.

When the results were analyzed, Alberta's achievement scores from the 2011 international TIMSS tests were the lowest in its history on that test for Grade 4 and Grade 8 students in mathematics. The international test (PISA 2009) in mathematics confirmed the decline as did Alberta's achievement on Canada's Pan-Canadian Assessment Program (PCAP) in 2010.

In reading, compared to the 2006 PIRLS, Alberta's international ranking slipped from first down to seventh because its reading score had declined by a statistically significant twelve points. Alberta was the only region that experienced such a significant decrease among the five Canadian provinces that participated in both 2006 and 2011 tests.

We concluded that the decline was due to the fact that there was a significant influx of new teachers into Alberta's schools combined with a substantial decline in teachers with more than twenty years of experience resulting in a significant decline in student achievement. *Alberta's experience illustrates why the current practice of providing teachers with incremental salary increases during the first five to ten years is inappropriate.* Experience does not provide a statistical increase in effectiveness until one has taught much longer. Therefore, a different model for providing teachers a pay bonus is required.

It is noteworthy that there is no research supporting the merits of the current grid system. Why do we persist in funding a system that is not providing a return on investment? *Is it possible we are so enslaved to tradition that facts no longer guide our reasoning and logic our decision making?* Is the alternative worrisome to unions because value regarding job performance will be assessed based on student outcomes?

With the evidence now available, it is indefensible to continue using the pay grid approach built on certification and years of experience. Jensen and Reichl (2011) get to the nub of the issue by stating the "implication is that all teachers with the same experience *are paid as though they are equally effective and improve at the same rate.*"

As long as this practice persists, the system will be more focused on a special interest group that is intended to serve rather than on the group to be served, namely the students. Perpetuating the status quo demonstrates we are more interested in currying the favor of a politically powerful employee than we are the client. This, in turn, demonstrates the self-centeredness of our politicians who seek reelection by pandering.

Union opposition toward pay-for-performance programs is fierce and the more intense their opposition the more clearheaded and wise we need our politicians to be. At some point, all of them are likely required to make a choice: *will they work with a group that is likely strong enough to elect them or will they work for the student who is essentially defenseless and certainly incapable of delivering votes on election day.* It takes political courage to change course and head in a different direction.

How does a politician overcome this "catch-22" situation? In a word, it is through *transparency*. In a political world where the fifteen-second sound bite is so dominant in our media, hard work is required to provide a rationale for political positions. Like a crown prosecutor in the court of law, the philosophical case for coming to a conclusion must be carefully outlined for the jury. Diligent preparation and hard work is required to educate the public so that it looks beyond the opposition of a special interest group.

The *politically safe* approach used too frequently is to listen only to the employees and their representatives without acquiring an understanding of what lies beneath the surface of their argument. Being knowledgeable requires a lot of data digging and asking difficult questions. Helping others to become knowledgeable requires hard work and risk taking. *More than anything, it requires politicians to begin the public discussion and courageously demonstrate, as once written on Starbucks' coffee cups, "On the battlefield of ideas, winning requires moving toward the sound of the guns."*

KEY POINTS

- Teachers' pay is based on inputs and not outcomes, although performance is being integrated in parts of the United States.
- Merit pay, an earlier form of performance pay, failed because it involved principals' subjective assessments, which then pitted teachers against each other.
- Research does not support basing teachers' pay on years of experience or certification.
- Overcoming this fallacious pattern requires politicians to engage in open, public discussion.

Chapter 15

Holding Parents Accountable

The education of our nations' children requires teamwork between parents and educators, with teachers taking the lead. This book is predominantly about holding educators more accountable because the school is primarily responsible for students' academic achievement. Including a chapter a few decades ago about holding parents accountable would have been absurd and, indeed, cockamamie; however, today's family is suffering a significant setback, making too many teachers play the role of surrogate parents.

Schools today are grappling with out-of-control absenteeism, student misbehavior, or poor follow-through in meeting the schools' expectations related to student learning. These examples of poor parenting prevent our schools from winning their oft-stated mission about excellence in student achievement. The severity of the negative impact these problems have on our schools should produce some form of political response but this remains relatively muted because governments fear voter backlash.

Students are the victims in this culture so devoted to political correctness, but their rights are *deemed secondary because they do not have power in the voters' booth*. Nor should they because their lack of maturity is insufficient to understand the complex issues facing our society. Therefore, it is incumbent on our leaders to make the needs of our young a greater priority than what is currently evident.

An adult workplace will not tolerate the bizarre situations increasingly evident in our children's worksite. Consequences are applied quickly when adults are noncooperative or threatening; yet, our students are deterred from making their best efforts because teachers are too frequently dealing with disruptive situations in their classrooms. Principals have too few options available for controlling the more severe misbehaviors.

Parents, unfortunately, answer to no one. Even their supposedly legal obligation to have their child in school until a specific age is, for too many, a requirement beyond their capacity to deliver. Laws written to control such irresponsibility are "toothless tigers" because *follow-through on the consequences does not exist.* Our society needs stronger political leadership to ensure that allowing a segment of the school population to foist their ignorance upon others is not the norm.

Truancy, for example, is an important matter in parental responsibility that is easily quantified. Strauss (2011) writes:

> In a last-ditch effort to curb out-of-control truancy levels, many states have decided that punishing the parents of chronically absent kids is an appropriate response. In Maryland, some parents have been jailed for failing to bring their kids to school. Parents in Alaska can be fined up to $500 for every five unexcused absences, and California passed a law allowing them to prosecute, fine, and jail parents in similar situations.

Some lawmakers are responding to the escalating truancy problem by hitting people in their wallets or putting them in jail. Is this harsh? Are these consequences realistic in our civilized society? Definitely controlling significant behavioral issues such as attendance and cooperation make these consequences valid after the school has demonstrated reasonable effort to ameliorate problems. Compulsory community service is an additional consideration before invoking incarceration, especially when this mandatory service is publicly published. Principals must be entrusted to refer deficient parenting to an accessible body without layers in between and with legal authority to take action.

If these consequences are deemed outlandish, what others might be employed for achieving higher levels of parenting? How we deal with inappropriate conduct in the workplace might be an appropriate response for guiding our use of consequences when dealing with parents *who bring children into our world and then absolve themselves of their responsibilities.* Our society feels justified that fines and incarceration are civilized means to penalize people who are unwilling to meet societal expectations. The significant issue is whether our politicians possess the necessary will to validate these consequences by following through when circumstances warrant.

Consequences is a word frequently shunned because it connotes negativity but positive actions are also consequences—letters of commendation, "A" or "excellent" on report cards, plaques for distinguishing service, bonuses, etc. Good teaching and parenting involves constant use of praise and recognition to reinforce children and it is axiomatic that *what we do for children we should also use with adults.*

Report cards on student learning and effort are distributed several times a year and a *similar method can be used with parents*. A large school district recently communicated with this writer—a principal there at one time—regarding an innovation recognizing good parenting. *Every reporting period, many handwritten letters of appreciation were appended to report cards of respectful students in each class.*

The experience of having parents "beat-down the principal's door" expressing their appreciation for such recognition was gratifying to the writer but equally rewarding to teachers who could remind their students of their obligation to maintain high standards. Decades later, this district has many principals using this simple task for recognizing and reinforcing good parenting.

The critical point is that providing parents with feedback on their parenting is important and the school's perceptions are important because teachers see the impact of parenting more than anyone. *The current situation and worsening trend warrants formalizing feedback into a report from the school* Therefore, providing parents a *year-end report card* is appropriate and maintaining this record in the student's file is more so. The summary should incorporate a *grading scale* with four or five levels and include issues such as the following:

- Parent attendance at parent-teacher conferences
- The child demonstrating respectful behavior toward the staff and school
- Parent(s) accepting suggestions for improving their child's academic success and following through with commitments
- The child attending regularly and arriving punctually
- Parent(s) providing volunteer service in their child's school

Reporting on parenting is not an approach that should be implemented haphazardly within only a few schools in a region. Parental malpractice is a societal concern and politicians must endorse reporting so that *parents understand that schools are expected to conform.* A child's education requires a partnership involving both school and home, and considerable progress is being made to hold schools accountable.

This book is primarily focused on increasing accountability at the school level and this chapter indicates some examples of how society is attempting to deal with more serious parent malpractice. The jump between doing nothing and using extreme methods of fining and incarcerating is too big and requires some intermediary actions, and they need to be objective and used routinely. The politically correct response of doing nothing and hoping the problem disappears is insufficient because the symptoms are too extensive.

This approach of providing parents with their schools' perception of parenting for effective education can be more palpable if the school system provided a quid pro quo for parents. Teacher evaluation processes frequently exclude parental input unless there is a serious issue. *Parents are clients of the school system and deserve to have input regarding the quality of service provided.* Therefore, including parents' perceptions about the quality of services that their child receives demonstrates *reciprocal accountability* for a service we deem essential in *learning well, living well.*

Doing nothing remains the significant issue for governments wanting to avoid "rocking the boat." For too long, avoidance has been the politically correct response on a social issue that is negatively impacting our school system and minimizing the critical partnership necessary for our children's success today and our society's well-being tomorrow.

A 2002 report issued by the Southwest Educational Development Laboratory (SEDL) synthesized fifty-one different studies on parent involvement in education. The report concluded that *students with involved parents are consistently more likely to achieve higher grades and test scores, continue on to some type of higher education and have better social skills, regardless of their socioeconomic background* (Puccinelli, 2015).

The important role parents fulfill is validated but the will to ensure our children benefit from their actions is not. Achieving a winning education system requires political action seemingly contrary to what our governments think is correct. Definitely inaction motivated by fear of losing some votes is no longer viable because, as this generation of students passes through the school system, the majority will follow their parents' poor practice with their own children.

SUGGESTIONS FOR EFFECTIVE PARENTING

The need for parent accountability is now so great that it overshadows providing a list of activities parents can undertake to be more effective in their role. Some suggestions routinely distributed by this author for parents seeking to enhance their child's schooling are:

1. Tell your child's teacher that you will not believe what your child says about that teacher if (s)he does not believe what is said about the parent. (Problems have many points of view and these are best discussed person to person.)
2. Schedule and keep a daily time for reading with younger children.
3. Make certain that your child "catches" both parents in the act of reading for pleasure.

4. Expand your child's vocabulary with a new word every week and ensure its daily use.
5. Never ask, "What did you learn today?" unless your child is beyond saying, "Nothing!"
6. Build relationships with the parents of your child's friends because it "takes a village to raise a child."
7. Avoid saying, "I was never good at math." This gives your child an excuse to follow your footsteps. Rather, think about activities at home where your child can solve mathematical problems.
8. Eat as a family and discuss issues and current events.
9. Model conflict resolution for your child.
10. Nurture relationships between your child and someone slightly older with "star qualities."
11. Monitor your child's use of the internet.
12. Establish a weekly schedule for watching television and reading.

KEY POINTS

- Today's family is suffering a significant setback adding the role of surrogate parent to too many teachers.
- Consequences for parental malpractice are necessary.
- Parent accountability is achievable through use of a parenting report card which can be more palatable by allowing parental input into teacher evaluations.

Chapter 16

Reducing Unfairness to Students

Assessing student work is an important aspect of effective teaching, and accurately evaluating students' assignments is the foundation for fairness to students. Students' marks have profound implications for progressing through the school system, qualifying for scholarships, placement in prestigious universities and colleges and, ultimately, career opportunities with commensurate income. In essence, marks are the students' currency.

The *greatest threat to fairness comes from inconsistent marking* and chapter 4 documents the degree to which marks are inflated. This pernicious problem disadvantages students because their work effort declines from an unrealistic understanding of their success, and parents are less inclined to provide assistance when their child appears to be doing well in their school work even though this is not the case.

Unfairness is exacerbated by grade inflation, which is *not universally and equally applied.* Some students benefit more than others because their compliant behavior is rewarded with bonus points awarded subliminally. Equally troublesome is the advantage female students receive because their tendency toward compliancy is greater than their male colleagues (Dueck, 2014). Studies demonstrating inconsistent marking are overwhelmingly persistent and more troublesome because of the lack of evidence refuting these conclusions.

Standardized assessment including *anonymous marking* is the most preferred solution for achieving fairness but is controversial because it opens the door to *comparability*. Teachers are anxious about having student success measured by such assessment practices because student gains can then be used to quantify a teacher's performance.

Relying exclusively on standardized testing has been explored in various countries; however, teachers generally rebel against this apparent lack of trust. A politically correct environment bows to this complaint from such a large segment of the voting population and avoids standardized tests for every grade or for most grades. Teachers' marks then provide the basis for determining students' grades with all of the attendant problems previously indicated.

Ensuring that classroom teachers are not the *only marker* of their students' work is a partial solution to this conundrum. Teachers, serving as critical friends, mark *subjective assignments* for each other's class, and these pairings should not be within the same schools. Students' *anonymity* is a must for ensuring fairness because bias will creep into assessments when the student's identity is known. A stringent commitment for anonymity is a significant reason in adopting system-wide testing. Fairness to all students is compromised when teachers have even the slightest amount of information about the student whose work is being assessed.

This process of assessing students' work using the marks of the classroom teacher and a colleague at the same grade level but from a different school should not be used haphazardly. The majority of subjective assignments should be handled in this fashion because fairness is the primary consideration, and achieving this purpose is worth the time and effort expended.

Teachers report that their professional development from discussing differences in perceptions during group assessments of students' work is their most valuable experience (Dueck, 2014). For example, a 1993 report to the US Congress regarding the strengths of Alberta's education system focused on how valuable the involvement of teachers was during the marking process where any identity of students was not available. This report concluded:

> In 1990-91, 500 Alberta teachers were involved in developing, piloting, or *serving on scoring panels* for one English examination taken by 24,000 students. (In other words, one teacher was involved for every 48 students targeted for the examination).... Widespread teacher involvement ... helps increase teachers' knowledge of curricula and instruction and aids in the development of tests that are compatible with good classroom instruction.
>
> In contrast, U.S. teachers do not typically play key roles in the development of commercial or state tests and, thus, *do not have access to similar experiences that hold the promise of improving both teaching and testing."*

This report to Congress was focused on the value of system testing in which teachers are involved in every aspect. This chapter recognizes that many governments lack in their commitment for ensuring fairness to students and, therefore, that an element of fairness can still be transferred into a flawed school system. Anonymous marking provided by one or more teachers increases fairness in assessments and facilitates higher levels of professional development. The politically correct route is to place teachers atop the pyramidal pinnacle because they can vote.

Schools and districts can achieve higher levels of fairness when governments fail to provide a process for ensuring consistent, accurate, and fair assessments of student learning. Banding together classes and schools where the same tests at the end of semester or year are used provides opportunity for marking students' responses anonymously. Fairness increases when each student's response is marked by at least two teachers and, when the marks differ by more than 20 percent, involving a third evaluation.

KEY POINTS

- The greatest threat to fairness for students comes from inconsistent marking.
- Grade inflation is a significant problem exacerbated by it not being universally applied.
- Teachers can improve their capacity to assess by involving other teachers when marking their students' work and then comparing and discussing differences.
- Schools and districts can enhance fair assessments even when governments fail to ensure accountability.

Chapter 17

Meeting the Costs

Learning well, living well is a dominant mindset in this book because North America's economic well-being depends on how well our next generation of workers is educated. A politically correct environment followed by governments worldwide is threatening economic ruin for many countries leading to financial hardships for many citizens. In Canada, for example, every citizen's (including babies) share of national debt is more than $17,000 and in the United States almost $61,000. State or provincial debts add to these incredulous amounts. Citizens worldwide should study the financial conditions of countries by Googling "debt clocks" that demonstrate debt in individual countries.

Books rather than a paragraph can and should be written about this predicament; however, this issue regarding government debt is raised because of politicians' foolishness while pandering for votes from special interests. Debt produces interest charges which "eat away" our capacity to *live well* because governments are unable to sustain programs and services. Canadians, for example, pay approximately $50 billion as annual interest for federal and provincial government debt and the *average taxpayer* contributes $2,300 annually toward this horrific debt, which would build many hospitals, schools, roads, bridges, water mains, etc. across the country.

American *citizens' annual payments* on the interest are approximately $7,500. This is wasted spending because it is on borrowed money. Our governments have followed the path of least resistance where "throwing money" at issues was the easiest way to capture votes. In other words, they simply did our bidding and violated Thomas Jefferson's fundamental moral and economic principle that *loading up the nation with debt and leaving it for the following generations to pay is morally irresponsible. Excessive debt is a means by which governments oppress the people and waste their substance. No nation has a right to contract debt for periods longer than the majority contracting it can expect to live.*

Education is a major spender of taxpayers' dollars and, therefore, this book concludes with some significant conclusions regarding government spending. First and foremost, every political body responsible for education should remain within its budget or hold accountable its politicians by recovering money spent beyond a balanced budget with a *special levy on these undisciplined spenders.* Specifically, the first dollars required to cover a deficit comes from the politicians in government until 25 percent of their government salary is confiscated. Thereafter, citizens would be on the hook as we now are.

Accountability is an investment and not an expense. Introducing some pressure into the school system improves results more than pouring in huge amounts of funding. Some reforms require specific funding for launching and/or maintaining impetus; however, educators become so attached to existing programs and few are ever culled. Therefore, *education does not suffer from inadequate funding but is plagued by misplaced expenditures.*

We have already indicated that class size reduction is a working condition rather than a learning condition and, when financial reductions become necessary, we should expect that education's workforce will have to work harder as is the case within the private sector. Yes, rolling back on this issue is difficult because of the political connotations; yet, our economic realities cannot sustain a bloated public sector: budget reductions will become a reality.

Significant savings are also available through implementing the birth-month option proposed in chapter 7. Eliminating approximately two-thirds of all student retentions as well as the many remediation costs presents huge budget savings in both capital and ongoing operational costs.

Recommendations herein propose lengthening of the school day and year, which requires negotiations to resolve the teachers' unions clever ploy at confusing the public. Can teachers legitimately equate their annual salaries to others in either the private or public sectors, who do not receive thirteen weeks of vacation? Class size and birth-month programming provide ample opportunity for governments to achieve fair settlements, which place students atop the pyramidal pinnacle.

Most of the remaining recommendations provided in this book are relatively cost-neutral because they are policy issues more than programming. *The point of this brief chapter is to emphasize that transforming education is not dependent on additional tax dollars* but is achievable by governments doing what they should do: making difficult decisions with a mindset that learning well will help us live well.

Jean Monnet's famous quote reminds us, however, that logic in the public arena is not anymore inevitable than it is in our private lives: "People only accept change in necessity and see necessity only in crisis." School districts rarely want to be truly reformed because the ruling class of any system never wants to reform anything that reduces its power and authority, although they say they do. This book is intended to motivate reform by helping define and publicize the crisis within education in the hope that students truly are first in our thinking.

Summary of Recommendations

- Politicians should be held to the same standard of accountability as a Grade 1 child by developing report cards measuring governments' performance on educational outcomes. (Ch. 3)
- Check-and-balance measures should be implemented to standardized testing by implementing teachers' perceptions of each student's academic success in *reading* and *mathematics* by using *grade level of achievement* (GLA). (Ch. 3)
- The procedures available when system leaders apply consequences and hold organizations accountable should be articulated in advance. (Ch. 3)
- A common assessment to achieve comparability and accountability should be implemented. (Ch. 4)
- Governments should expand choice by supporting private schools and charter schools. (Ch. 5)
- Parents should be encouraged to place their child in a public school they believe is more aligned with their child's needs. (Ch. 5)
- School districts should provide transportation for students to other schools where space permits. (Ch. 5)
- Teacher evaluations should be conducted by someone outside of the school freeing the principal to coach and providing opportunity for district staff to engage in instructional leadership. (Ch. 6)
- A dual-entry approach should be implemented to reduce by half the students' age spread in instructional groupings. (Ch. 7)
- Participants approved for funding to professional development conferences external to their district should commit to providing service within their district upon their return. (Ch. 8)

- School district workshops should conclude with an evaluation of the session and its presenter, which are rolled into a rating on the district report card. (Ch. 8)
- Staff expectations should include identifying annual professional improvement plans incorporating measurable outcomes. (Ch. 8)
- Principals and teachers should annually participate in peer observations concluding with informal discussions with their supervisor. (Ch. 8)
- Staff autonomy for planning a school's professional development program should be curtailed when student outcomes are not improving. (Ch. 8)
- The US education system has very high expenditures for school district administration and will benefit from district amalgamations. (Ch. 9)
- The number of school days for students should be increased by renegotiating the school year as the students' work year. (Ch. 10)
- The school system should address the educational needs of students who have fallen behind by lengthening the existing school day. (Ch. 10)
- The current school year should be extended beyond two hundred days so that North American children have the requisite skills and knowledge to compete in the global economy. (Ch. 10)
- Teachers' unions should not have the right to make union membership mandatory for the right to teach. (Ch. 11)
- Monopolistic enterprises, such as teaching, should not be able to use strikes as a weapon in negotiating collective agreements. (Ch. 11)
- Performance pay should be sent to teachers' unions when students' outcomes on the system report card warrant. (Ch. 11)
- Legislated "progressive discipline" for poor performance ratings on the system report card should include teachers' union leadership. (Ch. 11)
- A common standards approach for teacher preservice should be developed, if not nationally then state or province-wide. (Ch. 12)
- System-wide standardized assessments for teacher training programs should be implemented to evaluate trainee learning and publicly report results. (Ch. 12)
- The system of training institutions should be required to develop common policies for assessing preservice teachers using a mark quota system with a minimum of five gradings. (Ch. 12)
- School districts should be required to complete a standardized assessment evaluating each new graduate's teaching talent and publicly report results by institution and program—for example, elementary, secondary, fine arts, etc. (Ch. 12)
- First-year teachers receiving "less than satisfactory" evaluations should collect on their "warranty" from their certifying institution with free upgrading. (Ch. 12)

Summary of Recommendations 175

- Teacher tenure, or job-for-life, should be replaced with term-specific contracts with the length of terms conditional on the teacher's assessed level of performance. (Ch. 13)
- Teachers' pay should not be based on years of experience and certification but on gains made in student outcomes. (Ch. 14)
- A stronger school-home partnership should be achieved by having the school provide a report card on the level of support received from the home and providing parents the opportunity to provide input on the quality of services provided in their children's class.
- Fair assessments of students' work require a marking process where student anonymity is ensured, and schools should be obligated to ensure that a process for anonymous marking is in place. (Ch. 16)
- The first dollars required to cover a budget deficit should come from the politicians' personal funds until 25 percent of their government salary is confiscated. (Ch. 17)

References

Adler, J. "Debate: Are Teachers' Unions the Problem—or the Answer?" *Newsweek*, March 18, 2010.
Aiger, A. "Five Domains for Early Childhood Development." *Livestrong.com.* April 15, 2015.
Allen, J. "Accountability Lies at the Heart of Charter School Success" *(Press release). Center for Education Reform*, March 2009.
Anderson, J. "Curious Grade for Teachers: Nearly All Pass." *New York Times*, March 30, 2013.
Anderson, K. "The Number of US Children Living in Single-Parent Homes Has Nearly Doubled in 50 Years: Census Data." *Lifesitenews.com.* January 24, 2013.
Babcock, P. "Real Costs of Nominal Grade Inflation? New Evidence from Student Course Evaluations." *Economic Inquiry* 48, no. 4, October 2010.
Baker, A. "Many New York City Teachers Denied Tenure in Policy Shift." *New York Times*, August 17, 2012.
Bamesberger, M. "Nebraska's Master's Degree Bonuses for Teachers May Need Refiguring." *Daily Nebraskan*, February 3, 2011.
Barber, M., and M. Mourshed. *How the World's Best-Performing School Systems Come Out On Top*. New York: McKinsey and Company, 2007.
Barth, P., and R. Mitchell. "Standardized Tests and Their Impact on Schooling: Q&A." www.centerforpubliceducation.org, February 16, 2006.
Bennett, P. "A Well-Kept Secret: Whatever Happened to Canada's Charter Schools?" *Our Kids The Trusted Source*, April 10, 2010.
Bishop, J. H. *High School Exit Examinations: When Do Learning Effects Generalize?* Cornell University, jhb5@cornell.edu, 2005.
Black, C. "Public-Sector Unions Are a Blight On Our Society." *National Post*, May 4, 2013.
Buddin, R., and G. Zamarro. "Teacher Qualifications and Student Achievement in Urban Elementary Schools." *Journal of Urban Economics*, Vol. 66, No. 2, September 2009.

Caruth, D., and G. Caruth. "Grade Inflation: An Issue for Higher Education?" *TOJDE* 14, no. 1, Article 9, January 2013.

Center for Teaching Excellence, "Improving Your Test Questions." www.cte.illinois.edu (accessed June 21, 2011).

Clemens, J., M. Palacios, J. Lover, and F. Fathers. "Measuring Choice and Competition in Canadian Education: An Update on School Choice in Canada." *Fraser Institute*, February, 2014.

Crowley, B. "Public Sector Workers Should Not Have the Right to Strike." *Ottawa Citizen*, January 10, 2013.

Darling-Hammond, L., R. Chung Wei, A. Andree, and N. Richardson. "Professional Learning in the Learning Profession: A Status Report on Teacher Development in the United States and Abroad." Oxford, OH: National Staff Development Council, 2009.

Dillon, S. "Top Test Scores from Shanghai Stun Educators." *The New York Times*, December 7, 2010.

Dillon, S. "Teacher Grades: Pass or Be Fired." *The New York Times*, June 27, 2011.

Dueck, J. *Being Fair With Kids*. New York: Rowman & Littlefield Publishers, Inc., 2013.

Dueck, J. *Education's Flashpoints*. New York: Rowman & Littlefield Publishers, Inc., 2014.

Dueck, J. *Common Sense about Common Core*. New York: Rowman & Littlefield Publishers, Inc., 2016.

Education Insights. "Reality Check 2006—Issue No. 3: Is Support for Standards and Testing Fading?" www.publicagenda.org, 2006.

Elliott, P., and J. Agiesta. "AP-NORC Poll: Parents Back High-Stakes Testing." Associated Press-NORC Center for Public Affairs Research website, August 17, 2013.

Farkas, S., J. Johnson, and A. Duffett. *Stand by Me*. New York: Public Agenda, 2003.

Fitzgerald, S. "Teachers Unions Target Charter Schools." *Newsmax*, April 16, 2013.

Fullan, M. *The Moral Imperative of School Leadership*. Thousand Oaks, CA: Corwin Press, Inc., 2003.

Fullan, M. *Leadership and Sustainability*. Thousand Oaks, CA: Sage Publications, 2005.

Fullan, M. "Positive Pressure." *Springer International Handbooks for Education*, 23(1), pp. 119–30, 2009.

Garrett, R. "What Is Teacher Tenure?" www.education.com, accessed December 30, 2010.

Gerstner Jr., J. "The Tests We Know We Need." *New York Times*, March 14, 2002.

Gewertz, C. "Only 8 Percent of Students Complete College- and Career-Ready Curriculum." *Education Week*, April 5, 2016.

Gladwell, M. *Outliers*. New York: Little, Brown and Company, 2008.

Gladwell, M. *David and Goliath*. New York: Little, Brown and Company, 2013.

Goe, L., and L. M. Stickler. "Teacher Quality and Student Achievement: Making the Most of Recent Research." *TQ and Policy Research Brief*, 2008.

Greenberg, J., A. McKee, and Walsh, K. "Teacher Prep Review. National Council on Teacher Quality, December 2013.

Greene, J. P. *Education Myths.* New York: Rowman & Littlefield Publishers Inc., 2005.

Haney, W. "Evidence on Education under NCLB (and How Florida Boosted NAEP Scores and Reduced the Race Gap)." www.bc.edu, September 2006.

Hanushek, E., J. Kain, D. O'Brien, and S. Rivkin. *The Market for Teacher Quality.* NBER Working Paper No. 11154, February 2005.

Harris, D. N., and T. R. Sass. "Teacher Training, Teacher Quality, and Student Achievement." *National Center for Analysis of Longitudinal Data in Education Research,* March 2008.

Henninger, D. "The Fall of the House of Kennedy." *The Wall Street Journal,* January 21, 2010.

Howell, W., M. West, and P. Peterson. "The Public Weighs in on School Reform." *EducationNext,* fall 2011.

Hoxby, C. "Do Private Schools Provide Competition for Public Schools?" *NBER Working Paper Series 4978,* December (National Bureau of Economic Research), 1994.

Hoxby, C. "The Cost of Accountability." www.nber.org, April 2002

Hughes-Jones, D., C. Alexander, Z. Rudo, D. Pan, and M. Vaden-Kiernan. *Teacher Resources and Student Achievement in High-Need Schools Research Report.* January 2006.

Jensen, B., and J. Reichl. *Better Teacher Appraisal and Feedback: Improving Performance.* Melbourne: Grattan Institute, 2011.

Jensen, B., J. Sonnemann, K. Roberts-Hull, and A. Hunter. "Beyond PD: Teacher Professional Learning in High-Performing Systems, Australian Edition." Washington, DC: National Center on Education and the Economy, 2016.

Juel, C., G. Biancarosa, D. Coker, and R. Deffes. "Walking with Rosie: A Cautionary Tale of Early Reading Instruction." *Educational Leadership* (2003), 60, 12–18.

Knowles, T. "The Trouble with Teacher Tenure: We Can't Make Progress If Bad Teachers Have Jobs for Life." *The Wall Street Journal,* June 18, 2010.

Koedel, C. "Grade Inflation for Education Majors and Low Standards for Teachers." *American Enterprise Institute,* No. 7, August 2011.

Laurie, L. "Grade Inflation Sets Up Students to Fail: Study." *Halifax,* Nova Scotia: Atlantic Institute for Marketing, 2007.

Lawson, H. "Girls Get Higher Marks at School Than Boys Because They Are Better Behaved." *Daily Mail Online,* April 1, 2013.

Layton, L. "GOP-Led States Increasingly Taking Control from Local School Boards." *Washington Post,* February 1, 2016.

Leaks Sr., S. *It's Time Truth Speaks.* Xulon Press, 2010.

Leung, M. "Private Sector Workers Earn Less, Work More: Report." CTVNews.ca, March 23, 2015.

Lurie, S. "Why Doesn't the Constitution Guarantee the Right to Education?" *The Atlantic,* October 16, 2013.

McCombs, J. S., S. N. Kirby, and L. T. Mariano. *Ending Social Promotion Without Leaving Children Behind: The Case of New York City.* Santa Monica, CA: RAND Corporation, 2009.

McGuinn, P. "Ringing the Bell for K-12 Teacher Tenure Reform." www.americanprogress.org, February 2010.

Mellon, E. "HISD Moves Ahead on Dismissal Policy." *Houston Chronicle*, January 14, 2010.

Mitchell, R. "A Guide to Standardized Testing: The Nature of Assessment." www.centerforpubliceducation.org, February 15, 2006.

Mourshed, M., C. Chijioke, and M. Barber. "How the World's Most Improved School Systems Keep Getting Better." ssomckinsey.darbyfilms.com, November 2010.

Newberger, E. *The Men They Will Become: The Nature and Nurture of the Male Character*. Perseus Publishing, 1999.

Niels, G. "Top Reasons Why Students Cheat." About.com Guide, January 17, 2014.

Peterson, P., W. Howell, and M. West. "Teachers' Unions Have a Popularity Problem." *Wall Street Journal*, June 4, 2012.

Peterson, P., S. Barrows, and T. Gift. "After Common Core, States Set Rigorous Standards." *Education Next*, summer 2016.

Phelps, R. "Estimating the Costs and Benefits of Educational Testing Programs." www.education-consumers.com, February 2002.

Phelps, R. *Kill the Messenger: The War on Standardized Testing*. Transaction Publishers, 2003

Phelps, R. "The Effect of Testing on Achievement: Meta-Analyses and Research Summary, 1910–2010." *Nonpartisan Education Review*, April 2011.

Public Agenda, "Where's the Backlash? Students Say They Don't Fret Standardized Tests." www.publicagenda.org, March 5, 2002.

Puccinelli, M. "Holding Parents Accountable." *The Blue Review*, May 6, 2015.

Ravitch, D. *The Death and Life of the Great American School System*, 2010.

Rebarber, T., and A. Zgainer. *Survey of America's Charter Schools 2014*. The Center for Education Reform, 2014.

Reeves, D. *Accountability in Action: A Blueprint for Learning Organizations*. Advanced Learning Centers, Inc., 2000.

Rhee, M. "Rhee-forming D.C. Schools," www.wsj.com, accessed November 22, 2008.

Rhee, M. "Rhee-Forming D.C. Schools." www.education.com, accessed December 30, 2010.

Roza, M., and R. Miller. "Issue Brief: Separation of Degrees." *Generation Progress*, July 21, 2009.

Sands, A. "Education Minister Aims to Kickstart Talks with New Offer to Alberta Teachers." *Edmonton Journal*, February 22, 2013.

Scholastic and the Bill and Melinda Gates Foundation. "Primary Sources: America's Teachers on America's Schools." www.scholastic.com, March 2010.

Slavov, S. "How to Fix College Grade Inflation." *U.S.NEWS*, December 26, 2013.

Strauss, V. "Holding Parents Accountable: Grades? Fines? Jail?" *The Washington Post*, June 8, 2011.

Tobias, S. "School Consolidation Could Save Money, but Critics Worry About Other Costs." *The Wichita Eagle*, January 28, 2016.

Tompson, T., J. Benz, and J. Agiesta. "Parents' Attitudes on the Quality of Education in the United States." *The Associated Press-NORC Center for Public Affairs Research*, 2013.

Troyan, M. "Major Rewrite of Education Law Clears Crucial Hurdle." *USA Today*, November 20, 2015.

US Department of Education. "Testing: Frequently Asked Questions." www.ed.gov, November 17, 2004.

Vu, P. "Do State Tests Make the Grade?" *www.stateline.org*, January 17, 2008.

Walberg, H. "Stop the War Against Standardized Tests." *Defining Ideas*, May 2011.

Webber, C., N. Aitken, J. Lupart, and S. Scott. *The Alberta Student Assessment Study*. The Crown in Right of Alberta, 2009.

Weisberg, D., S. Sexton, J. Mulhern, and D. Keeling. *The Widget Effect*. The New Teacher Project, 2009.

Xiang, Y., M. Dahlin, J. Cronin, R. Theaker, and S. Durant. "Do High Performing Students Maintain Their Altitude?" *Performance Trends of Top Performing Students*. Thomas B. Fordham Institute, September 20, 2011.

Xueqin, J. "The Test Chinese Schools Still Fail." *Wall Street Journal*, December 8, 2010.

Yeh, S. "Limiting the Unintended Consequences of High-Stakes Testing." *Education Policy Analysis Archives*, October 28, 2005.

Yoon, K., T. Duncan, S. Lee, B. Scarloss, and K. Shaplee. "Reviewing the Evidence on How Teacher Professional Development Affects Student Achievement." *National Center for Education Evaluation and Regional Assistance*, 2007.

Zwaagstra, M. C., R. A. Clifton, and J. C. Long. "Getting the Fox Out of the Schoolhouse: How the Public Can Take Back Public Education." *Atlantic Institute for Market Studies*, 2007.

About the Author

Jim Dueck, EdD, has had a career in education spanning forty years of service as a teacher, principal, superintendent, and assistant deputy minister. He also advised representatives from approximately fifty educational systems around the world who sought suggestions regarding assessment and accountability in education, including the US government's launching of the Race to the Top initiative. In 2016, he was identified by the US Department of Education as one of three experts to share expertise in accountability nationally. He also has authored three previous books: *Being Fair with Kids*, *Education's Flashpoints*, and *Common Sense About Common Core*.

www.ingramcontent.com/pod-product-compliance
Lightning Source LLC
Chambersburg PA
CBHW052121300426
44116CB00010B/1753